Reading ADVENTURES

1

Carmella Lieske • Scott Menking

HEINLE
CENGAGE Learning

Australia • Brazil • Japan • Korea • Mexico • Singapore • Spain • United Kingdom • United States

Reading Adventures 1
Carmella Lieske, Scott Menking

Publisher: Andrew Robinson

Executive Editor: Sean Bermingham

Senior Development Editor: Derek Mackrell

Assistant Editor: Claire Tan

National Geographic Editorial Coordinator:
  Leila Hishmeh

Director of Global Marketing: Ian Martin

Assistant Marketing Manager: Anders Bylund

Content Project Manager: Tan Jin Hock

Senior Print Buyer: Mary Beth Hennebury

Compositor: Page 2, LLC.

Cover/Text Designer: Page 2, LLC.

Cover Photo: Carsten Peter/National Geographic
  Image Collection

Acknowledgments

The Authors and Publishers would like to thank
the following teaching professionals for their
valuable feedback during the development of
this series.

Lewis Berksdale, Kanazawa Institute of Tech-
nology, Japan; Clare Chun, Language World,
Korea; **John Dennis**, Hokuriku University, Japan;
Kátia Falcomer, Casa Thomas Jefferson, Brazil;
Alexandra Ruth Favini, Escuela Graduada
"Joaquin V. Gonzalez," Argentina; **Yuka Iijima**,
Dokkyo University, Japan; **Pia Isabella**, Colegio
Nacional "Rafael Hernández" UNLP, Argentina;
Minkyoung Koo, Woongin Plus Language
School, Korea; **Alison Larkin**, Box Hill Col-
lege, Kuwait; **Laura MacGregor**, Gakushuin
University, Japan; **Jill Pagels**, KAUST Schools,
Saudi Arabia; **Hyunji Park**, Kyunghee Univer-
sity, Korea; **Stephen P. van Vlack**, Sookmyung
Women's University, Korea; **Deborah Wilson**,
American University of Sharjah, United Arab
Emirates

Library of Congress Control Number: 2011937606

ISBN-13: 978-0-8400-2841-9

ISBN-10: 0-8400-2841-5

Heinle
20 Channel Center Street
Boston, MA 02210
USA

Cengage Learning is a leading provider of customized learning solutions with
office locations around the globe, including Singapore, the United Kingdom,
Australia, Mexico, Brazil, and Japan. Locate your local office at
www.cengage.com/global

Cengage Learning products are represented in Canada by Nelson Education, Ltd.

Visit Heinle online at **elt.heinle.com**

Visit our corporate website at **www.cengage.com**

Printed in the United States of America
3 4 5 6 7 16 15 14

Contents

Get Ready for an *Adventure!*

A grizzly bear in Alaska really loves her brother. How did she help him? **p. 27**

NORTH AMERICA

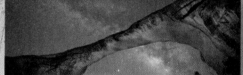

What is a Dark Sky Park? **p. 89**

A menu from the ship *Titanic* is worth a lot of money. How much? **p. 49**

SOUTH AMERICA

FLORIDA

LOTTO WINNER

Sheelah Ryan

$ 2,767,361

September 7, 1988

NON-NEGOTIABLE

Sheelah Ryan was very, very lucky. Why? **p. 65**

This frog is very dangerous. Why? **p. 85**

What were the first Olympics like? **p. 105**

The Great Pyramid is a wonder of the world. Who made it, and how? **p. 43**

David went to the Beijing Olympics. What did he see? **p. 101**

EUROPE

ASIA

AFRICA

October 25, 2010 was a terrible day for the people near Mt. Merapi, Indonesia. Why? **p. 13**

David Fisher has an idea for a new building. Why is it special? **p. 49**

Before 1950, some Chinese men and women had a terrible job. What did they do? **p. 39**

AUSTRALIA

ANTARCTICA

Ian Nichols and his family lived in Gabon. What was it like? **p. 23**

The sundew is a very special plant. Why is this plant unusual? **p. 75**

Scope and Sequence

Unit Walkthrough

▲ Robot fish from the Massachusetts Institute of Technology, U.S.A.

Warm Up
discussion questions introduce the unit topic.

Warm Up

Talk with a partner.

1. Can you think of some important inventions? Make a list.
2. Imagine you can invent anything. What does your invention do?

47

Before You Read tasks
encourage students to think about the ideas in the reading.

4A A New Building

Before You Read

A **Discussion.** Look at the photos of the building above. What is special about it? Discuss with a partner.

B **Definitions.** Match the words with their meanings.

| 1. speed | 2. shapes | 3. slow | 4. energy |
| 5. machine | 6. sound (v.) | 7. impossible | 8. human |

_____ a. ■ ▲ ●
_____ b. something like a computer or a car
_____ c. When something is _____, no one can do it.
_____ d. Every man, woman, and child is a(n) _____.
_____ e. When things _____ good, they seem to be good.
_____ f. The _____ of something is how fast it moves.
_____ g. not fast
_____ h. the power or strength to do things

48 Unit 4 Big Ideas

Reading

Strategy: Scanning. Who had the idea for this building?

The architect wants to ▶ build the new building in Dubai. This is the view from the top of Dubai's tallest building.

The Building That MOVES

Everyone knows that buildings don't move. They can't change the way they look. However, architect[1] David Fisher wants to change that.

Fisher has an amazing idea. He wants to make **80-story** buildings that change **shape**. Each floor will move around **slowly**. The floors will move at different **speeds**. Because of this, the shape of the building is always changing. "These buildings will never look the same," says Fisher.

His idea is an interesting one. However, Fisher doesn't stop there. He also wants the building to be "green."[2] The building will make its own **energy**. In most buildings, only the top floor has a roof.[3] In Fisher's building, each floor will have its own roof. The roofs each have solar panels.[4] This means a lot more solar energy. Also, **machines** between each floor of the building will catch the wind. They will turn the wind into energy.

Fisher's ideas **sound impossible**. However, that's what people also said before **humans** traveled into space!

¹ an **architect** designs buildings
² **green:** good for the environment

³·⁴ a **roof** with ▲ solar panels

49

Reading Passages
are adapted and graded from authentic sources.

Reading Comprehension
questions check students' understanding of the reading passage.

Reading Comprehension

A Circle the correct answer.

Gist 1. Another title for this reading is _____.
   a. A Building for the Future
   b. The Life of an Architect
   c. How Green Buildings Work

Vocabulary 2. In line 3, **80-story** means the building has 80 _____.
   a. shapes   b. floors   c. different speeds

Detail 3. Fisher's building makes a lot of solar energy because the building _____.
   a. is always moving   b. is very tall   c. has many solar panels

Purpose 4. Why does the writer say "that's what people also said before humans traveled into space?"
   a. to show why Fisher's building will never work
   b. to show why Fisher's building is like a spaceship
   c. to show that unusual ideas can sometimes work

B **Strategies: Labeling.** Look at the picture below. Complete the labels using words from the passage.

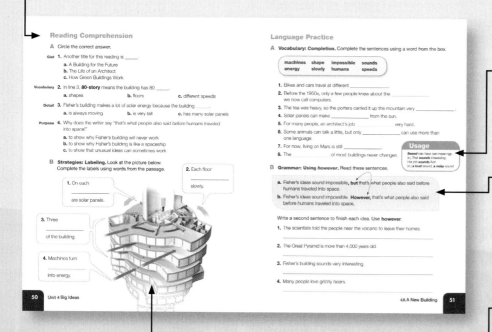

1. On each _____ are solar panels.

2. Each floor _____ slowly.

3. Three _____ of the building.

4. Machines turn _____ into energy.

50 Unit 4 Big Ideas

Language Practice

A **Vocabulary: Completion.** Complete the sentences using a word from the box.

| machines | shape | impossible | sounds |
| energy | slowly | humans | speeds |

1. Bikes and cars travel at different _____.
2. Before the 1950s, only a few people knew about the _____ we now call computers.
3. The tea was heavy, so the porters carried it up the mountain very _____.
4. Solar panels can make _____ from the sun.
5. For many people, an architect's job _____ very hard.
6. Some animals can talk a little, but only _____ can use more than one language.
7. For now, living on Mars is still _____.
8. The _____ of most buildings never changes.

Usage

Sound can have two meanings.
(v.) *That* **sounds** *interesting.*
He (*n.*) **sounds** *fun!*
(n.) *a loud* sound, *a noisy* sound

B **Grammar: Using however.** Read these sentences.

a. Fisher's ideas sound impossible, **but** that's what people also said before humans traveled into space.
b. Fisher's ideas sound impossible. **However**, that's what people also said before humans traveled into space.

Write a second sentence to finish each idea. Use **however**.

1. The scientists told the people near the volcano to leave their homes.
_____

2. The Great Pyramid is more than 4,000 years old.
_____

3. Fisher's building sounds very interesting.
_____

4. Many people love grizzly bears.
_____

4A A New Building 51

Vocabulary Builder
boxes highlight common collocations, affixes, and usage notes.

Grammar activities
practice important grammar structures introduced in the reading passage.

Maps, charts, and diagrams help students
develop visual literacy.

Reading Strategies give students the practice and support they need to be better readers.

Before You Read tasks introduce eight target vocabulary items from the reading.

Target Vocabulary items from the readings are identified in blue.

Reading Comprehension questions include question types commonly found in international exams, such as TOEIC®, TOEFL®, and IELTS®.

4B Big Ideas, Small Sizes

This **solar-powered light** is useful for places with no electricity.

The **baby warmer** is an inexpensive way of keeping babies warm.

The **chili grinder** helps people grind hot chillies without hurting their hands.

Before You Read

A **Discussion.** Some good designs can help people around the world. Look at the pictures. Why are these inventions good? Talk about your ideas with a partner.

B **Definitions.** Match the words with their meanings.

1. probably 2. both 3. clean 4. roll 5. sick 6. easy 7. last (v.) 8. repeat

____ a.
____ b. do again
____ c. not dirty
____ d. When something will ____ happen, it is likely to happen.
____ e.
____ f. two things
____ g. not hard to do.
____ h. When things ____, they don't stop or break.

52 Unit 4 Big Ideas

Reading

Strategy: Skimming. Quickly read the passage. Who are these inventions for? Tell a partner.
a. people without clean water
b. people in the U.S.
c. people with a lot of money

Making It Safe

1 Do you drink water every day? Is it clean? You **probably** answered yes to **both** questions. But 900 million people around the world don't have safe drinking water. Without **clean** water, they get **sick** more easily.
5 That's why these two ideas are so great! They can make a big difference for a lot of people.

The LifeStraw

This straw cleans water when you drink through it. It is small and **easy** to carry. You can get clean water
10 anywhere you go. It **lasts** over six months for most people. You don't have to worry about getting a new **one** often.

The Q Drum

This new **container** helps people carry clean water to their homes.
15 In rural places, people often have to walk to get clean water. Then they have to carry it back to their homes. They **repeat** this every day they need water, but water is heavy. You don't have to lift the Q Drum. You can **roll** it home. No more carrying 50 kilograms of water!

53 4B Big Ideas, Small Sizes

Reading Comprehension

A Circle the correct answer.

Detail 1. The passage says that 900 million people ____
a. need clean water   b. use the LifeStraw   c. carry water to their homes

Reference 2. In line 12, the word **one** refers to ____.
a. a straw   b. a container   c. water

Vocabulary 3. Which of these is a **container** (line 14)?
a. a chair   b. a box   c. a knife

Inference 4. The writer probably thinks ____.
a. carrying water is very easy for most people
b. the straw is more useful than the container
c. most people don't really think about their water

B **Strategy: Classification.** Which invention(s) do these sentences describe. Write a to f in the correct place.

a. It helps people have clean water.
b. You can carry it.
c. It's easy to use.
d. It is heavy, but you can roll it.
e. It helps people take water to their homes.
f. It helps people get sick.

Q Drum   LifeStraw

both

54 Unit 4 Big Ideas

Language Practice

A **Vocabulary: Words in context.** Share your answers with your partner.

1. What are some times when you **repeat** what someone says?
2. What are some things you can **roll**?
3. What do you think is popular now but **probably** won't be popular in a year?
4. What do you do when you are **sick**?
5. What do **both** your mother and father like to do?
6. Do you think studying English is **easy**?
7. Give an example of something that **lasts** more than a year.
8. How often do you **clean** your room?

B **Grammar: have to / don't have to.** Read these sentences from the passage.

a. You **don't have to** worry about getting a new one soon.
b. In rural places, people often **have to** walk to get clean water.
c. Then they **have to** carry it back to their homes.
d. You **don't have to** lift the Q Drum.

Complete each sentence using **have to / don't have to** so they are true for you. Compare answers with a partner.

Usage
Use **have to / don't have to** with I, you, we, or they.
Use **has to / doesn't have to** with he, she, or it.

1. I ____ walk to school every day.
2. I ____ make my own lunch every day.
3. On Sunday I ____
4. In my English class we ____

55 4B Big Ideas, Small Sizes

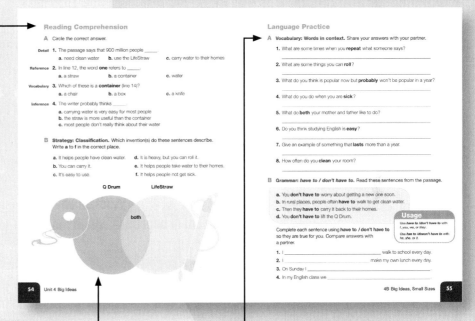

Reading Comprehension questions include question types commonly found in international exams, such as TOEIC®, TOEFL®, and IELTS®.

Graphic organizers help students understand the organization of the text and the connections between key ideas.

Vocabulary sections practice and reinforce target vocabulary from the reading.

Video
Solar Cookers

A **Preview.** Look at the pictures and label the different ways of cooking food.

electricity   gas
solar energy   woodfire

1
2   3   4

B **As you watch.** Choose True (T) or False (F) for each sentence.
1. Bob Metcalf is a cook.   T F
2. SCI shows people how to use solar energy.   T F
3. When the WAPI's wax melts, people can drink the water.   T F
4. Before solar cookers, most of the women in the video cooked using gas.   T F

C **Think about it.** How is solar cooking better for the Earth than other ways of cooking?

56 Unit 4 Video

Video activities give extra comprehension and vocabulary practice, and motivate students to learn more about the unit topic.

Review Unit Walkthrough

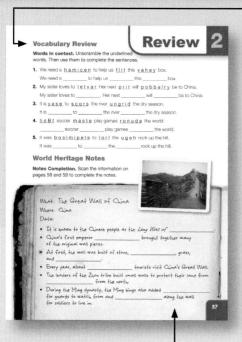

Vocabulary Review

activities reinforce the vocabulary from earlier units.

World Heritage Site

pages highlight important cultural and natural places around the world, and recycle vocabulary and structures from earlier units.

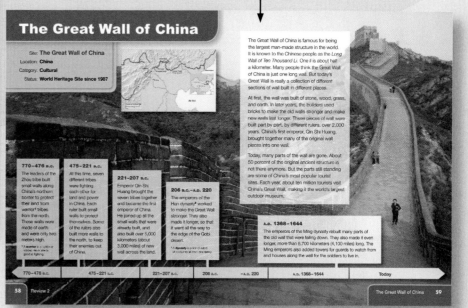

World Heritage Notes preview content of World Heritage Site pages.

Folktales from areas related to the World Heritage sites in the preceding spread introduce students to stories from cultures around the world.

Reading Comprehension

questions check students' understanding of the folktale.

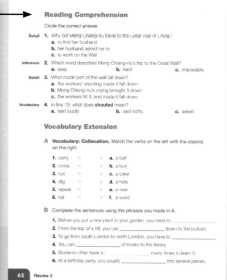

Make reading an adventure online—anywhere, any time! Visit **www.HeinleELT.com/readingadventures** for self-study grammar, vocabulary, and reading activities. Watch the National Geographic videos from the series either inside or outside the classroom.

Volcanoes

A volcano erupts in Sicily, Italy. ▲

Warm Up

Talk with a partner.

1. What volcanoes do you know?
2. What words describe a volcano? Make a list.

1.

2.

Indonesia

▲ Mount Semeru (top) and Mount Bromo (left with smoke)
are two volcanoes in Indonesia.

Before You Read

A Labeling. Read the paragraph. Then use the words in **blue** to label the picture.

A **volcano** looks like a mountain, but active volcanoes sometimes erupt. There are about 1,900 active volcanoes in the world. Before volcanoes erupt, **smoke** and ash come out of them. When a volcano erupts, hot lava comes out.

B Definitions. Match the words (**1** to **8**) with their meanings (**a** to **h**).

1. hot   **2.** air   **3.** happy   **4.** near   **5.** terrible   **6.** safe   **7.** leave   **8.** a lot of

_____ **a.** close to, not far

_____ **b.**  🙂

_____ **c.** go out from, go away from

_____ **d.** many

_____ **e.**

_____ **f.** not dangerous

_____ **g.** the thing we breathe

_____ **h.** very, very bad

Reading

Strategy: Scanning. When did Mount Merapi erupt? How many times did it erupt that day?

Mount Merapi Erupts

1   For the people near Mount Merapi—a volcano in Indonesia—Monday, October 25, 2010 started like
5   every other day. People got up. They went to school and work. Like many other days, smoke and ash[1] came out of the volcano. Before this, scientists[2] told the people **near** the mountain to **leave** their homes. However, **they** didn't want to leave. That morning, the volcano was worse. The scientists again told people to
10 leave their homes. This time the people went to a **safe** place.

Mount Merapi erupts.

Monday Afternoon

That afternoon, Mount Merapi erupted three times. **Hot** lava and rocks went
15 down the mountain. **A lot of** ash went into the **air**. Because of the ash, people could not see the mountain.

After the Eruption

After the eruption, people went
20 back to their homes. There was ash in their rooms. There were no trees or other plants. It was **terrible**. The people were very **happy** they left their homes
25 before the eruption.

▲ [2] Some **scientists** look at volcanoes. They are called *volcanologists*.

▲ [1] **Ash** on plants near Mount Merapi.

Reading Comprehension

A Circle the correct answer.

Gist **1.** What is the reading mainly about?

    a. people near Mount Merapi   **b.** an eruption   **c.** volcanoes in Indonesia

Detail **2.** When did the scientists first tell people to leave Mount Merapi?

    a. before October 25   **b.** on October 25   **c.** after October 25

Reference **3.** In line 8, the word **they** means _____.

    a. scientists   **b.** the people   **c.** the homes

Purpose **4.** The purpose of the third paragraph is to tell us _____.

    a. about the problems from the eruption
    b. what the scientists did next
    c. why the volcano erupted

B **Strategy: Sequencing.** Number the events in order from **1** to **5**.

    a. _____ The people near Mount Merapi left the mountain.

    b. _____ The people went back home.

    c. _____ Ash went into the people's rooms.

    d. _____ Mount Merapi erupted three times.

    e. _____ Scientists told people to leave the mountain.

Mount Merapi (left) ▼

Language Practice

A   Vocabulary: Completion. Complete the sentences using a word from the box.

> a lot of   air   happy   hot   leave   near   safe   terrible

1. All people need _____ to live.

2. In the U.S., most people _____ high school when they are about 18.

3. Indonesia is _____ Malaysia.

4. Indonesia has _____ islands—more than 15,000!

5. We often say "_____ Birthday!" on a person's birthday.

6. It is not _____ to go too near an erupting volcano.

7. In 1883, a(n) _____ eruption on Krakatoa, Indonesia, killed more than 40,000 people.

8. Most deserts[1] are _____.

[1] a **desert**

Usage

A lot of means *very many* or *very much.*
A lot is also an adverb: *I like him a lot.*

B   Grammar: Parts of a reading passage. Write the correct numbers to label the parts of the reading passage.

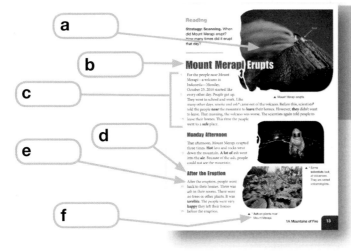

a   b   c   d   e   f

1. title   **4.** picture
2. subheading   **5.** caption
3. paragraph   **6.** sentence

In each sentence below, circle the best answer.

1. The title of the passage is (**Mount Merapi Erupts** / **Monday Afternoon**).

2. There are (**2** / **3**) subheadings in the passage.

3. There are (**3** / **4**) paragraphs in the passage.

4. There are (**2** / **3**) pictures with captions on page 13.

5. The last paragraph has (**4** / **5**) sentences.

Journey to the Center of the Earth

Jules Verne (1828–1905) was a writer of science-fiction and adventure ▶ books. Two of his books are *Twenty Thousand Leagues under the Sea* and *Around the World in Eighty Days*. He also wrote the book *A Journey to the Center of the Earth* in 1864.

Before You Read

A Discussion. Read the information below. What do you think Axel and Professor Liedenbrock are going to do?

The passage on the next page is from *A Journey to the Center of the Earth*. In the story, two men, Axel and Professor Liedenbrock, find a book with a secret message. The secret message was from a man called Arne. It tells of Arne's journey deep into a volcano.

B Definitions. Match the words with their meanings.

> **1.** beautiful   **2.** climb   **3.** imagine   **4.** inside   **5.** sudden   **6.** rest   **7.** deep   **8.** whole

_____ **a.** all of something

_____ **b.** fast and surprising

_____ **c.** think about

_____ **d.** move up or down a mountain

_____ **e.** not outside

_____ **f.** very far down

_____ **g.** stop work and don't do anything

_____ **h.** very good to look at

Iceland

Reading

Strategy: Skimming. Read the passage quickly. Did the volcano erupt? **Yes / No**

INTO THE VOLCANO

1 We stood at the top of Mount Sneffels in Iceland. This was the volcano Arne went into. Now it was our turn to go **inside**!

From the top, I looked out and I could see the **whole** island. It was **beautiful**. Then I looked down, **deep** into the volcano. Did Arne really go in there? There was no
5 time to think about that. It was time to go!

Down, down, down we **climbed**. The climb was very hard, but in the afternoon, we were at the bottom. I sat down to **rest**. I **imagined** the volcano **suddenly** erupting, with rocks, ash, and lava coming out. "**This** is a terrible idea!" I thought, but the professor didn't seem to feel this way. He was very happy, and he ran **here and there**,
10 looking at everything. Suddenly, he called, "Axel, come here!" and pointed to the wall. On the wall, I could see the word *Arne*.

Reading Comprehension

A Circle the correct answer.

Detail **1.** Who was the first person into Mount Sneffels?

    a. Arne   **b.** Axel   **c.** the professor

Reference **2.** In line 8, the word **this** means _____.

    a. sitting down to rest   **b.** going into the volcano   **c.** seeing the volcano erupt

Vocabulary **3.** In line 9, **here and there** means _____.

    a. many different places
    b. around the island
    c. the top and bottom of the volcano

Inference **4.** In the story, how many people went down into the volcano (counting everyone)?

    a. 2   **b.** 3   **c.** 4

B **Strategy: Sequencing.** Read the story again. Put the pictures in order from **1** to **5**.

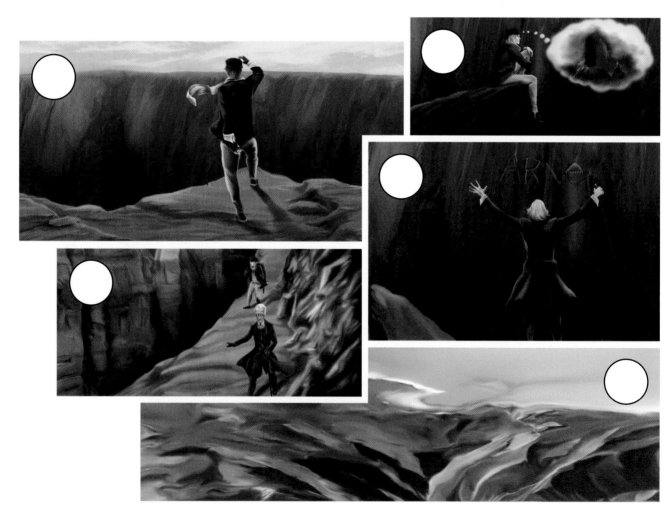

Language Practice

A Vocabulary: Matching. Match the two halves of the sentences. Then (circle) the numbers of the sentences you agree with. Compare your answers with a partner.

1. Most people can't **climb** __d__
2. Dogs and cats can _____
3. There is no way to _____
4. Most volcanoes _____
5. A person can eat _____
6. It is good to work all day _____
7. Your TV² is usually _____
8. Most people think _____

a. **suddenly** learn English.
b. a **whole** cake¹ in 10 minutes.
c. **inside** your home.
d. a very tall mountain.
e. mountains are **beautiful**.
f. without a **rest**.
g. are **deep**.
h. **imagine** things.

¹ a **cake**

² a **TV**

B Punctuation. Write the correct number(s) to complete the sentences.

exclamation point ❗
question mark ❓
period .
quotation mark "
comma ,

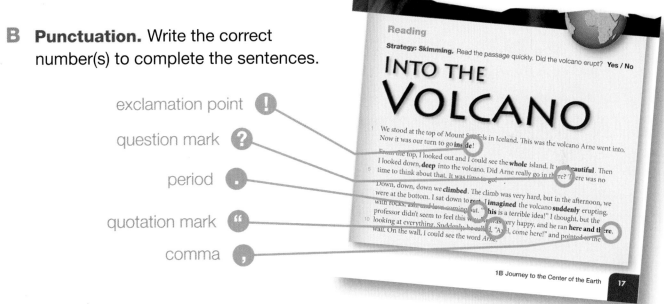

1. There are _____ periods in the second paragraph.
2. The passage has _____ commas.
3. The passage has _____ exclamation point(s) and _____ question mark(s).
4. There are _____ sentences in quotation marks in the passage.

Word Partners

Use **deep** with:
a deep **breath**, deep **water**, a deep **hole**,
deep **sleep**, a deep **voice**

Volcanoes

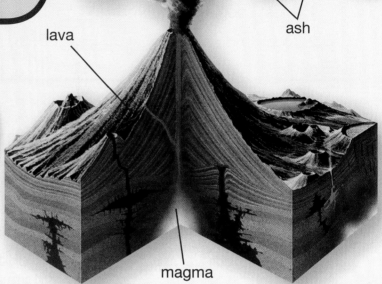

lava

ash

magma

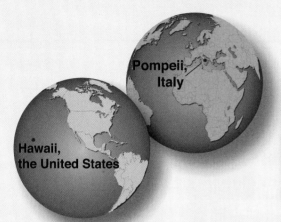

Pompeii, Italy

Hawaii, the United States

A Preview. Complete the information about volcanoes using the words in the box.

> erupt   lava   ash   magma

Inside the Earth, there is hot **1.** _____. Sometimes volcanoes **2.** _____ and magma comes out. When magma comes out of a volcano, the magma is called **3.** _____. Also, when a volcano erupts, **4.** _____ goes into the air.

B As you watch. Match the numbers to the correct sentences.

> 79   80   90   1,500   1983

1. About _____ of the volcanoes on Earth still erupt.

2. About _____ percent of all volcanoes are in the Ring of Fire.

3. In _____, Kilauea in Hawaii started erupting.

4. In A.D. _____, Mount Vesuvius erupted near Pompeii.

5. Volcanoes made _____ percent of the land.

C Talk with a partner. Did any of the sentences in **B** surprise you? Why?

Families

◄ A proboscis monkey mother and her baby sit in a tree in Sabah, Malaysia.

Warm Up

Talk with a partner.

1. How many people are in your family? What do they do?
2. How are animals' and people's families the same? How are they different?

2A My Family

1. _____

2. Ian's _____

3. _____

4. _____

5. Fidele

6. _____

7. Ian, Fidele's _____

▲ This is Fidele, a boy from Rwanda. He is showing a **picture** of his **friend**, Ian Nichols, and Ian's **family**. You can see Ian's **father**. His name is Michael. You can see his **mother**, too. Her name is Reba. Ian also has a **brother**, Eli. Eli was just a little baby then. Ian doesn't have a **sister**.

When Ian was a boy he went to school in Rwanda. In this picture, ▶ he is **studying** with his friends.

Rwanda

Gabon

Before You Read

A **Labeling.** Read about the two pictures above. Write the words in **blue** in the correct boxes. Two words are extra.

B **Definitions.** Match the words with their meanings.

1. brother **2.** family **3.** father (dad) **4.** friend
5. mother (mom) **6.** sister **7.** study (v.) **8.** take pictures

_____ **a.** a woman; she has children

_____ **b.** a girl; she has the same mother or father

_____ **c.** to learn

_____ **d.** brother, father, mother, and sister together

_____ **e.** a man; he has children

_____ **f.** a boy; he has the same mother or father

_____ **g.** a person you like

_____ **h.** to use a camera

Strategy: Scanning. Look at the passage. Circle the family words.

TO AFRICA WITH DAD

My first trip

My **dad** is a photographer so he goes all over the world and
takes pictures. For fifteen years, he went to Africa, most of the
time by himself. But when I was about 7, my dad took me and
my **mom**, Reba, to Rwanda. My dad took pictures, and I studied
with Rwandan students. We became good **friends**, and when
we weren't studying, we found amazing worms,[1] birds, and
other animals.

Back to Africa

I went back to Africa again when I was 22. My mother and
my **father** took me and my **brother**, Eli, with them to Gabon.
For six months, we camped in the grass near beautiful trees
and palms.[2] In the day, my father and I took pictures, and Eli
studied on the beach with my mom. At night we slept in our
camp, and the animals came near us.

My dad says Africa
with his family
was amazing.
I think so, too.

[1] a **worm**

▲ Ian Nichols
in Rwanda

▲ Eli Nichols
studying in his
family's camp
in Gabon

[2] a **palm tree**

Ian's father, Michael Nichols, ▶
took this photo of an elephant
in Africa.

Reading Comprehension

A Circle the correct answer.

Gist **1.** What is this passage mainly about?

    a. animals in Africa   **b.** how to take pictures   **c.** Ian Nichols and his family

Detail **2.** How old was Ian when he first went to Rwanda?

    a. 7   **b.** 14   **c.** 22

Detail **3.** Who studied in Gabon?

    a. Eli   **b.** Reba   **c.** Ian

Vocabulary **4.** A **camp** (line 15) is a place where you _____.

    a. sleep outside   **b.** take photos   **c.** go to school

B **Strategy: Sequencing.** Put these events in order. Write **a** to **d** on the timeline.

    a. Ian Nichols is born.   **c.** Ian's family goes to Gabon.

    b. Ian's family goes to Rwanda.   **d.** Mike Nichols usually goes to Africa alone.

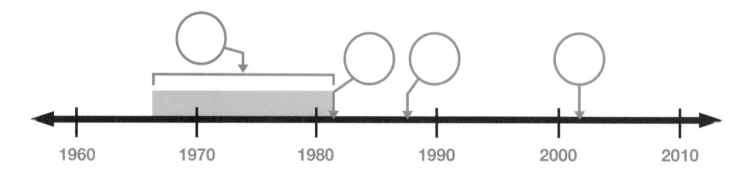

1960   1970   1980   1990   2000   2010

Ian Nichols and his ▶ father, Michael, in the Republic of the Congo in 2008

Language Practice

A **Vocabulary: Words in context.** Answer the questions below.

1. How many **brothers** do you have? _____

2. Who is the youngest person in your **family**? _____

3. What is your **father's** name? _____

4. How old is your best **friend**? _____

5. What is your **mother's** name? _____

6. Do you have a **sister**? _____

7. Do you **study** English every day? _____

8. Do you like to **take pictures**? _____

B **Grammar: Using *so* and *when*.** Read these two sentences.

> **a.** My dad is a photographer, **so** he goes all over the world and takes pictures.
>
> **b.** **When** I was about 7, my dad took me and my mom, Reba, to Rwanda.

Use **so** or **when** to join the sentences below.

1. Ian lived in Rwanda. He studied at a Rwandan school.

   _When_____

2. Africa is far from the U.S. It takes many hours to fly there.

   _____

3. The camp was outside. Animals came there at night.

   _____

4. Michael went to Gabon. He took many beautiful photographs.

   _____

> ### Word Partners
>
> Use *friend* with:
> (*adj.*) **best** friend, **close** friend, **good** friend, **old** friend
> (*v.*) **make a** friend

Animal Families

river

salmon

grizzly bear

teeth

▲ There are a lot of salmon in the rivers of Alaska, and bears love to **catch** them.

Bear mothers have one to four babies, called cubs, at one time. The cubs ▶ **stay** with their mother, and the mother **looks after** them until they are two years old. After that, the bears live **alone**.

Today, there are about 58,000 grizzly bears in North America. Many people **love** bears, but, sadly, some people hunt and **kill** them, and cut down their forests. Because of this, the bears are in **trouble**, and many people are **worried** about them. ▶

Alaska, the United States

Before You Read

A   Discussion. Read the information about bears above. What do you know about bears? Tell a partner.

B   Definitions. Match the words with their meanings.

> **1.** alone   **2.** catch   **3.** kill   **4.** look after
> **5.** love   **6.** stay   **7.** trouble   **8.** worry

_____ **a.** not with other people   _____ **e.** to not go

_____ **b.** problems   _____ **f.** really, really like

_____ **c.** to find and hold   _____ **g.** to take care of

_____ **d.** to make something die   _____ **h.** to think about bad things

Reading

Strategy: Skimming. Read the passage very quickly. What happened to the cub?

A Sister's Love

1   Do you think bears know who their brothers and sisters are? Do you think they love them in the same way people do?

Every summer, bears eat a lot of salmon. The grizzlies stand in the water and use their front legs[1] to feel the river bottom.[2]

5   When they feel a salmon, they **catch** it with their feet, and then **grab** it with their teeth.

[1] front legs

One young grizzly was having **trouble**. A hunter **killed** his mother and also shot the cub in the leg, so he could not fish. He tried and tried, but he never caught any salmon.

Stacy Corbin, a fishing guide[3] in Alaska, **worried** about the cub—until **he** saw the cub's

10   sister catch six salmon and put them near her brother's feet. While other cubs hunted **alone**, the sister **stayed** and **looked after** her brother. "She fed him for weeks," says Corbin. Because of her, he lived. That really is **love**!

[3] **fishing guide:** a person who shows people where to catch fish

▼ The bear's sister caught salmon for him until he was better.

[2] Salmon swim along the **river bottom**. ▶

27

Reading Comprehension

A Circle the correct answer.

Main Idea   **1.** What is the main idea of this passage?

    a. Grizzly bears are not very dangerous.
    b. Animals can feel love like people do.
    c. Hunting is a bad thing to do.

Detail   **2.** Why couldn't the cub catch fish?

    a. His mother was dead.   **b.** His leg was hurt.   **c.** He couldn't find fish.

Vocabulary   **3.** **Grab** (line 6) has the same meaning as _____.

    a. hold   **b.** kill   **c.** feel

Reference   **4.** On line 9, who is **he**?

    a. the hunter   **b.** Stacy Corbin   **c.** the cub

B   **Strategy: Identifying cause and effect.** Match the causes and effects to make sentences.

    1. A hunter shot a cub's mother, and   ○   ○   **a.** it couldn't catch fish.

    2. The bear's foot was hurt, so   ○   ○   **b.** it didn't die.

    3. The cub couldn't catch fish, so   ○   ○   **c.** Stacy Corbin thought it was in trouble.

    4. The cub's sister helped it, so   ○   ○   **d.** she died.

A mother bear catches a salmon for her cubs.

Language Practice

A **Vocabulary: Words in context.** Answer the questions below so they are true for you. Then tell a partner.

1. What things do you **love**? _____

2. Have you ever **caught** a fish? _____

3. What is something you are **worried about** now? _____

4. Do you prefer to go places or **stay** home? _____

5. Do you enjoy being **alone**? _____

6. Do you know anyone in **trouble**? Who? _____

7. Do you feel bad if you **kill** an insect?[1] _____

8. Have you ever **looked after** a baby? _____

[1] A ladybird is a kind of **insect**.

B **Grammar: Indirect questions.** Read these sentences.

a. Who **are** their brothers and sisters?

Do bears know who their brothers and sisters **are**?

b. What **do** bears eat?

Do you know what bears eat?

Write the questions below using **Do you know . . . ?**

1. What is his name?
Do you know _____

2. When is her birthday?
Do you know _____

3. How did the bear catch the fish?
Do you know _____

4. Why is the bear angry?
Do you know _____

5. What are the salmon doing?
Do you know _____

6. Where do salmon live?
Do you know _____

Word Partners

Use *trouble* with:
(*v.*) **run into** trouble, **have** trouble, **make** trouble, **cause** trouble
(*adj.*) **big** trouble, **real** trouble, **serious** trouble
(*prep.*) trouble **with**, **in** trouble

Cheetah vs. Gemsbok

Kalahari Desert

▲ a gemsbok   ▲ a cheetah

A Preview. Read the information. Then write the words in blue next to their definitions.

Gemsbok and cheetahs live in Africa. They live in the **desert**, so they have to move around a lot to look for food and water. Cheetahs sometimes **hunt** gemsbok. But gemsbok have two big **horns** on their heads, and are not easy to kill.

1. hard, pointed things growing on an animal's head _____

2. a place with little or no water, rain, or plants _____

3. to look for and catch something to eat _____

B After you watch. Answer the questions.

1. Why is the mother cheetah worried?
   a. She can't find food.
   b. She can't find her children.
   c. Her children are not safe near gemsbok.

2. When will the cheetah cubs leave their mother?
   a. when they're less than 12 months old
   b. when they're 18 months old
   c. when they're more than 24 months old

3. Why does the mother gemsbok run after the cheetahs?
   a. She wants them to go away.
   b. She wants to eat them.
   c. She's playing with them.

C Think about it. How did you feel about the video? Were you happy the gemsbok wasn't killed, or were you sad the cheetahs couldn't find food?

Vocabulary Review

A **Odd word out.** One word in each group is a different part of speech to the others. Circle the different words.

1. beautiful / happy / terrible / trouble
2. leave / catch / whole / kill
3. many / inside / near / outside
4. climb / deep / study / imagine
5. alone / sister / father / brother
6. air / river / salmon / suddenly
7. friend / mother / safe / family
8. look after / a lot of / be worried / take pictures

S	F	Y	A	L	W	V	A	E
A	S	U	D	D	E	N	L	Y
F	B	R	O	S	Z	O	O	S
E	B	D	P	J	H	E	N	V
D	I	E	J	W	O	I	E	J
T	E	T	R	O	U	B	L	E
D	W	K	H	K	M	A	N	Y
E	C	T	J	F	L	Q	F	Q
A	L	O	T	O	F	G	Z	R

B **Word search.** Now look for the words you circled, and circle them in the puzzle.

World Heritage Notes

Notes completion. Scan the information on pages 32 and 33 to complete the notes.

What: Mt. Kilimanjaro

Where: _____, Africa

Data:

- Mt. Kilimanjaro is the tallest mountain in _____. It's _____ meters high.

- The land around the mountain is _____ and dry.

- There is _____ on the top of the mountain.

- There are a lot of different plants and _____ in Kilimanjaro National Park.

- About 1,000 people _____ Mount Kilimanjaro every year.

Kilimanjaro

Site: **Kilimanjaro National Park**

Location: **Tanzania, Africa**

Category: **Natural**

Status: **World Heritage Site since 1987**

Tanzania

At 5,895 meters high, Kilimanjaro is the tallest mountain in Africa. It is also one of the largest volcanoes in the world. Africa is really hot and dry, but the top of Mt. Kilimanjaro has snow on it!

The snow turns into water and flows down the mountain, so there's a lot of water. Many types of plants and animals—like elephants and giraffes—live near the mountain. Kilimanjaro National Park is a safe place for these animals to live, and a good place for a lot of different plants to grow.

Today, Kilimanjaro is a very popular place to visit. About 1,000 people climb the mountain every year. Climbing is hard work, but you don't have to be a good mountain climber to climb Kilimanjaro. You only have to be healthy.

Kilimanjaro 1993

Kilimanjaro 2000

Tanzania is usually very hot, but the air at the top of Kilimanjaro is very cold. It's so cold that there are large areas of ice, called glaciers. Scientists now tell us that Kilimanjaro's glaciers are getting smaller. The glaciers are now 85 percent smaller than they were in 1912. Today, there is less than 2 square kilometers of ice on the mountain. Soon, Kilimanjaro may have no more snow, and then no more water.

What Does "Kilimanjaro" Mean?

No one knows where the name Kilimanjaro came from. Some people believe it comes from old Swahili words that mean "white, shining hill."

A Tanzanian Folktale
The Rabbit and the Well

1 Long ago, there was a small village in Tanzania. Many different animals lived there. There were elephants and lions. There were antelopes and rabbits. The giraffe was the king of all the animals.

One summer it was very hot. There was very little rain. Soon, the animals
5 did not have enough water to drink.

The giraffe called a meeting of all the animals. "What can we do?" he asked them. They decided to dig a well. The rabbit, however, did not want to do any work.

The animals dug a well—and the rabbit sat nearby, laughing. Soon they had
10 cool, clean water to drink. The giraffe said, "The rabbit did not help with this well. He cannot drink the water. Every day, one animal will guard the well."

The first day the elephant guarded the well. The rabbit walked up to him and gave him some honey. The elephant asked for more. The rabbit said, "OK, but first I have to tie your hands and legs. You will enjoy the honey
15 more this way." The rabbit tied up the elephant and jumped into the well. He drank water, and swam and laughed. Then he ran away.

The giraffe was very angry. The next day, he asked the antelope to guard the well. The rabbit came by and tricked him, too. He drank water and swam. He laughed at the antelope and then ran away.

20 Finally, it was the turtle's day to guard the well. The turtle climbed into the water and waited for the rabbit. The rabbit came and did not see any guards. He jumped in the water—and the turtle grabbed him. He took him to the king. The rabbit was in trouble.

After that, all the animals enjoyed their water in peace.

Reading Comprehension

Strategy: Sequencing. Number the events in the story on pages 34 and 35 from **1** (the first) to **8** (the last).

a. _____ It was very hot one summer.

b. _____ The animals dug a well.

c. _____ The rabbit laughed at the antelope.

d. _____ The animals enjoyed their water in peace.

e. _____ The turtle grabbed the rabbit.

f. _____ The rabbit tricked the elephant.

g. _____ There was not enough water to drink.

h. _____ The rabbit did not help dig the well.

Vocabulary Extension

Vocabulary: Phrasal verbs. Phrasal verbs—a verb + a preposition or adverb— are very common in English. Complete the sentences with the correct preposition from the box. Then circle the six phrasal verbs in the reading.

at	away	for	into	up	with

1. Cats love to climb _____ small places.

2. It is not good to laugh _____ people in trouble.

3. Some people often wait _____ the bus for more than 30 minutes.

4. In some countries, you tie _____ old newspapers and put them outside.

5. Small animals often need to run _____ from big animals.

6. When you have trouble with your homework, you should ask someone to help you _____ it.

Amazing Feats

▲ A power station worker in Hanford, U.S.A.

Warm Up

Talk with a partner.

1. A *feat* is a very hard thing to do. Can you think of any feats one person did?
2. Do you know anything amazing a group of people did together?

The Long, Hard Road

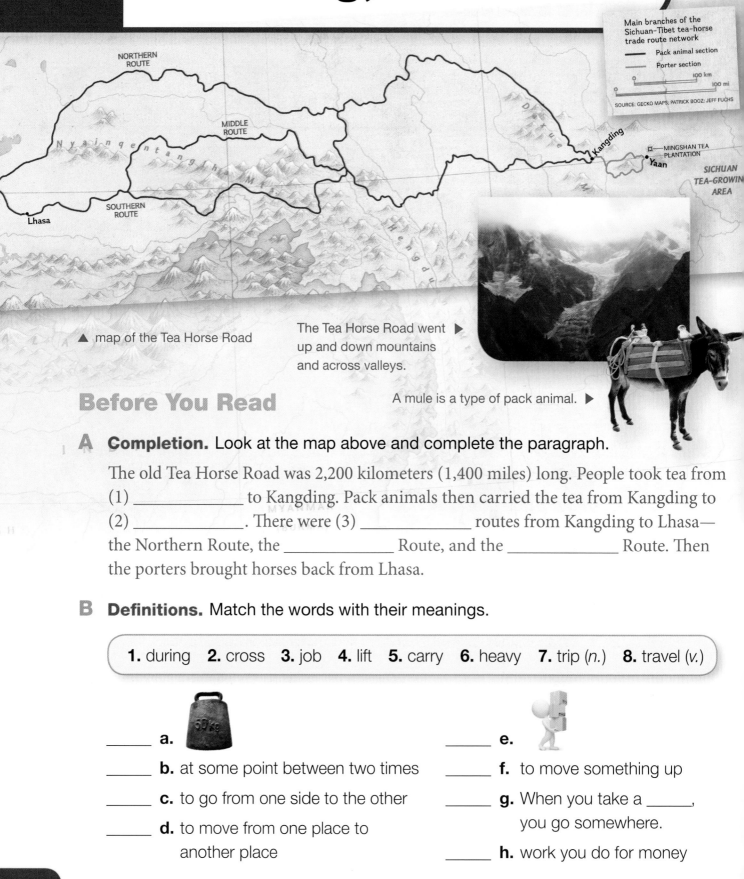

Main branches of the Sichuan-Tibet tea-horse trade route network

—— Pack animal section

—— Porter section

0 — 100 km
0 — 100 mi

SOURCE: GECKO MAPS; PATRICK BOOZ; JEFF FUCHS

NORTHERN ROUTE

MIDDLE ROUTE

SOUTHERN ROUTE

Lhasa

Kangding

MINGSHAN TEA PLANTATION

Yaan

SICHUAN TEA-GROWING AREA

▲ map of the Tea Horse Road

The Tea Horse Road went ▶ up and down mountains and across valleys.

A mule is a type of pack animal. ▶

Before You Read

A Completion. Look at the map above and complete the paragraph.

The old Tea Horse Road was 2,200 kilometers (1,400 miles) long. People took tea from (1) _____ to Kangding. Pack animals then carried the tea from Kangding to (2) _____. There were (3) _____ routes from Kangding to Lhasa— the Northern Route, the _____ Route, and the _____ Route. Then the porters brought horses back from Lhasa.

B Definitions. Match the words with their meanings.

> **1.** during   **2.** cross   **3.** job   **4.** lift   **5.** carry   **6.** heavy   **7.** trip (*n.*)   **8.** travel (*v.*)

_____ **a.**

_____ **b.** at some point between two times

_____ **c.** to go from one side to the other

_____ **d.** to move from one place to another place

_____ **e.**

_____ **f.** to move something up

_____ **g.** When you take a _____, you go somewhere.

_____ **h.** work you do for money

Reading

Strategy: Predicting. This passage is about people working on the Tea Horse Road. What do you think their job was like? Tell a partner.

PORTERS ON THE TEA HORSE ROAD

The tea porters are remembered in this statue park in Yaan, China.

▲ tea porters on the Tea Horse Road in 1908

1 Can you **lift** a person? Could you **carry** that person for 200 kilometers?

Before 1950, some Chinese did something like that. These men and women, called porters, carried tea on
5 their backs. They walked for 20 days. **During** that time, they **traveled** about 200 kilometers.[1]

Luo Yong Fu was one of the porters. Although he weighed only about 50 kilograms,[2] he carried more than 60 kilograms of tea! The **heavy** tea wasn't the only hard part
10 of the **trip**. The porters went up mountains. They **crossed** valleys. They didn't even stop when the snow was a meter deep. Luo Yong Fu carried tea from 1935 to 1949. He said, "It was a terrible **job**." But people today still remember their hard work. The horses they brought back helped many people in China.

The tea was heavy, so the porters had to rest often. As they walked, they sang a song.

15 ## THE PORTER'S SONG

Seven steps up, rest.
Eight steps down, rest.
Eleven steps flat, rest.
You don't rest, you are stupid.[3]

[1] **200 kilometers:** 125 miles
[2] **50 kilograms:** 110 pounds
[3] **stupid:** not clever or smart

Reading Comprehension

A Circle the correct answer.

Gist **1.** What is the reading mainly about?

    a. tea   **b.** tea porters   **c.** Luo Yong Fu

Detail **2.** Every day, the porters walked about _____ kilometers.

    a. 10   **b.** 20   **c.** 200

Detail **3.** Luo Yong Fu carried tea for about _____ years.

    a. 15   **b.** 35   **c.** 50

Purpose **4.** What is the purpose of the passage?

    a. to show how tea is carried today

    b. to show the history of tea in China

    c. to show the porters had a hard but important job

B **Strategy: Diagram completion.** Complete the diagram with the words from the box.

carry	cross	heavy	trip	travel

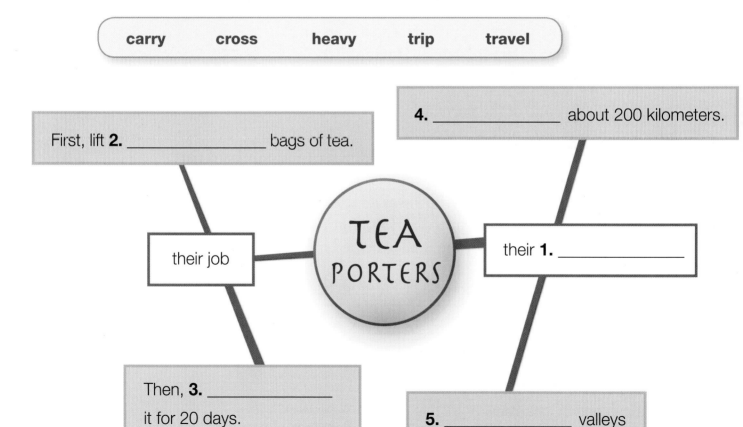

First, lift **2.** _____ bags of tea.

4. _____ about 200 kilometers.

their job

TEA PORTERS

their **1.** _____

Then, **3.** _____ it for 20 days.

5. _____ valleys

Language Practice

▲ [1] **The Great Wall** is over 8,000 kilometers long.

A Vocabulary: Words in context.
Circle the correct word in each sentence.

1. Students usually (**carry** / **lift**) their books in a bag.

2. You can't talk (**during** / **when**) tests.

3. Many birds (**trip** / **travel**) south in winter.

4. Firefighters have a hard (**work** / **job**).

5. (**Elephants** / **Insects**) are heavy.

6. Very few people can (**lift** / **trouble**) a car.

7. The Great Wall[1] (**crosses** / **travels**) China from east to west.

8. Some families take a (**trip** / **travel**) every year.

B Grammar: Contrasting using *although*. Read the example sentences. Sentence **b** is from the passage.

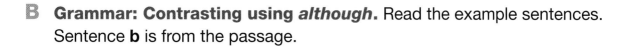

a. He weighed only about 50 kilograms, **but** he carried more than 60 kilograms of tea.

b. **Although** he weighed only about 50 kilograms, he carried more than 60 kilograms of tea.

Use **although** to join the sentences below. Then write two more sentences with your own ideas.

1. It was a terrible job. People still remember their hard work.

   _____

2. The tea was heavy. The porters carried it.

   _____

3. It often snowed. The porters didn't stop.

   _____

4. _____

5. _____

Word Partners

Use *cross* with:
cross **the street**, cross **a road**,
cross **a line**, cross **a river**

Building the Pyramids

▲ the pyramids of Giza, Egypt
The Great Pyramid is on the far left.

Egypt

Before You Read

A **Discussion.** Look at the picture above. How old are the pyramids? Who do you think built them? Talk about your ideas with a partner.

B **Definitions.** Match the words with their meanings.

> **1.** dig   **2.** mystery   **3.** perfect   **4.** cut
> **5.** huge   **6.** popular   **7.** team   **8.** around the world

_____ **a.** When something is _____, many people know and like it.

_____ **b.** in many different countries

_____ **c.** no problems, good in all ways

_____ **d.** something people cannot understand

_____ **e.**

_____ **f.**

_____ **g.** very, very big

_____ **h.** A group of people. They work together.

Reading

Strategy: Predicting. Look at the title and pictures. Check (✓) the question(s) you think the passage will answer. Then read and check your predictions.

☐ Who made the Great Pyramid?

☐ How did they make it?

☐ Where is it?

☐ How big is it?

▲ Egyptian workers carrying blocks to the Great Pyramid.

BUILDERS OF THE

PYRAMIDS

1 Every year, millions of people from **around the world** visit the Great Pyramid at Giza. It is as **popular** today as it was 4,000 years ago. During most of that time it was taller than any building on Earth.

How was it made?

Zahi Hawass ▶ (far right) is an Egyptian *archeologist*— he studies people of the past.

5 The Great Pyramid, one of the Wonders of the World, has more than 2 million blocks. Many of them are **huge**. Some are as heavy as five school buses! Although **they** were heavy, workers put a block into the pyramid every three minutes.

10 The workers, Egyptian men and women, worked in **teams**. The teams had different jobs. Some **dug** up the stones. Others moved them. Another team **cut** the stones. The last group put the stones into the pyramid.

The stone ▶ blocks in the Great Pyramid are huge.

15 Even though there were so many different teams, the pyramid is **perfect**. No stone is in the wrong place. But how did the Egyptians move those huge stones to the top? No one knows for sure. Some things are still a **mystery**.

Reading Comprehension

A Circle the correct answer.

Main Idea   **1.** The main idea of the third paragraph is _____ the builders worked.

     a. why   **b.** how   **c.** when

Reference   **2.** In line 8, the word **they** refers to _____.

     a. buses   **b.** workers   **c.** blocks

Detail   **3.** How many blocks did the workers put into the pyramid every hour?

     a. 1   **b.** 5   **c.** 20

Sequence   **4.** Which of the following happened last?

     a. Teams put the blocks into the pyramid.
     b. Egyptians moved the blocks up the pyramid.
     c. Workers cut the stones into blocks.

B   **Strategy: Notes completion.** Complete the notes below with one or two words from the passage.

The Great Pyramid
Millions of people (1) _____ every year.
More than (2) _____ years old.
For a long time was (3) _____ than any other building.

The blocks
More than (4) _____ of them.
Huge – as heavy as five (5) _____.
One put in the pyramid every (6) _____.

The workers
They worked (7) _____, each with a different job.
Some dug up (8) _____, and others moved them.
Another team (9) _____ them before they were put in the pyramid.

The pyramid today
Every stone is in the right place – the pyramid is (10) _____,
but how they moved the stones to the top is still (11) _____.

Language Practice

A **Vocabulary: Words in context.** In each sentence, circle the best answer. The words in blue are from the reading.

1. A **mystery** is something _____.   **a.** no one knows   **b.** all people know

2. A **huge** pyramid is very _____.   **a.** small   **b.** big

3. When something is **popular**, _____ people love it.   **a.** few   **b.** many

                                                                  [1] a **shovel**

4. A **team** sport has _____ person.   **a.** one   **b.** more than one

5. A **perfect** thing has _____ problems.   **a.** no   **b.** some

6. You use a _____ to **dig**.   **a.** shovel[1]   **b.** bag   [2] **glue**

7. We use _____ to **cut**.   **a.** a knife   **b.** glue[2]

8. When you travel **around the world**, you travel to _____.   **a.** safe places   **b.** many different countries

B **Grammar: Giving extra information.** Read these sentences; **a** is from the passage.

a. The pyramid has more than 2 million blocks. It is **one of the Wonders of the World**.
The pyramid, **one of the Wonders of the World**, has more than 2 million blocks.

b. Mount Merapi erupted on October 25. It is **a volcano in Indonesia**.
Mount Merapi, **a volcano in Indonesia**, erupted on October 25.

Join each pair of sentences to make one sentence. Then make two more sentences like these.

> ## Word Partners
>
> Use *popular* with:
> (*adv.*) **extremely** popular, **most** popular, **wildly** popular
> (*n.*) popular **culture**, popular **magazine**, popular **music**, popular **movie**

1. The Nile is the longest river in the world. It is a river in Egypt.

_____

2. Zahi Hawass is Egyptian. He is an archeologist.

_____

3. _____

4. _____

 **Video**

An Amazing Trip

Mali

A **Preview.** You will hear these words in the video. Use the words to complete the sentences.

> adult   journey   marry   thirsty   tribe

1. When you grow up, you become a(n) _____.
2. Most people in the U.S. choose for themselves the person they will _____.
3. The Fulani _____ lives in villages near the desert.
4. When you go on a(n) _____, you travel from one place to another, usually far away.
5. Someone who is _____ feels like they need to drink something.

B **As you watch.** Number the events in the correct order, 1–5.

a. _____   b. _____   c. _____

d. _____   e. _____

C **Think about it.** How are the Fulani culture and your culture different? How are they the same?

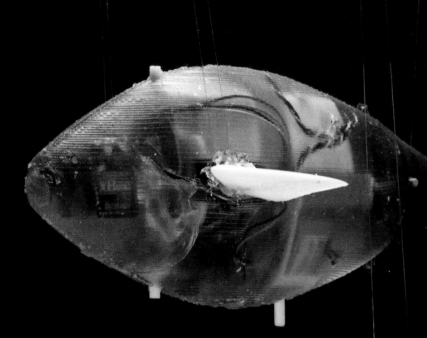

Big Ideas

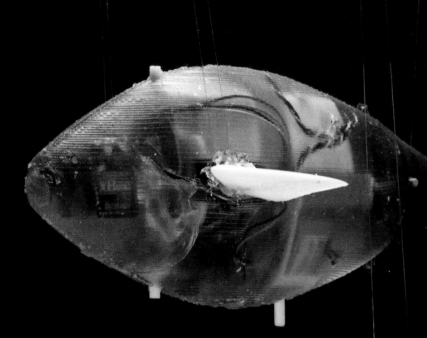

▲ Robot fish from the Massachusetts
Institute of Technology, U.S.A.

Warm Up

Talk with a partner.

1. Can you think of some important inventions? Make a list.
2. Imagine you can invent anything. What does your invention do?

Before You Read

A **Discussion.** Look at the photos of the building above. What is special about it? Discuss with a partner.

B **Definitions.** Match the words with their meanings.

1. speed	**2.** shapes	**3.** slow	**4.** energy
5. machine	**6.** sound (v.)	**7.** impossible	**8.** human

_____ **a.**

_____ **b.** something like a computer or a car

_____ **c.** When something is _____, no one can do it.

_____ **d.** Every man, woman, and child is a(n) _____.

_____ **e.** When things _____ good, they *seem to be* good.

_____ **f.** The _____ of something is how fast it moves.

_____ **g.** not fast

_____ **h.** the power or strength to do things

Reading

Strategy: Scanning.
Who had the idea
for this building?

_____

The architect wants to ▶
build the new building in
Dubai. This is the view from
the top of Dubai's tallest
building.

The Building That MOVES

1   Everyone knows that buildings don't move. They can't change the way they look.
    However, architect[1] David Fisher wants to change that.

    Fisher has an amazing idea. He wants to make **80-story** buildings that change **shape**.
    Each floor will move around **slowly**. The floors will move at different **speeds**. Because
5   of this, the shape of the building is always changing. "These buildings will never look
    the same," says Fisher.

    His idea is an interesting one. However, Fisher doesn't stop there. He also wants the
    building to be "green."[2] The building will make its own **energy**. In most buildings,
    only the top floor has a roof.[3] In Fisher's building, each floor will have its own roof.
10 The roofs each have solar panels.[4] This means a lot more solar energy. Also, **machines**
    between each floor of the building will catch the wind. They will turn the wind
    into energy.

    Fisher's ideas **sound impossible**. However,
    that's what people also said before **humans**
15 traveled into space!

[1] An **architect** designs buildings.
[2] **green:** good for the environment

[3, 4] a **roof** with ▶
solar panels

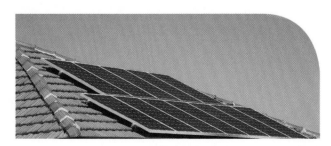

Reading Comprehension

A Circle the correct answer.

Gist **1.** Another title for this reading is _____.

    a. A Building for the Future
    b. The Life of an Architect
    c. How Green Buildings Work

Vocabulary **2.** In line 3, **80-story** means the building has 80 _____.

    a. shapes   **b.** floors   **c.** different speeds

Detail **3.** Fisher's building makes a lot of solar energy because the building _____.

    a. is always moving   **b.** is very tall   **c.** has many solar panels

Purpose **4.** Why does the writer say "that's what people also said before humans traveled into space!"

    a. to show why Fisher's building will never work
    b. to show why Fisher's building is like a spaceship
    c. to show that unusual ideas can sometimes work

B **Strategies: Diagram labeling.** Look at the picture below. Complete the labels using words from the passage.

2. Each floor

_____

slowly.

1. On each

_____

are solar panels.

3. Three

_____

of the building.

4. Machines turn

_____

into energy.

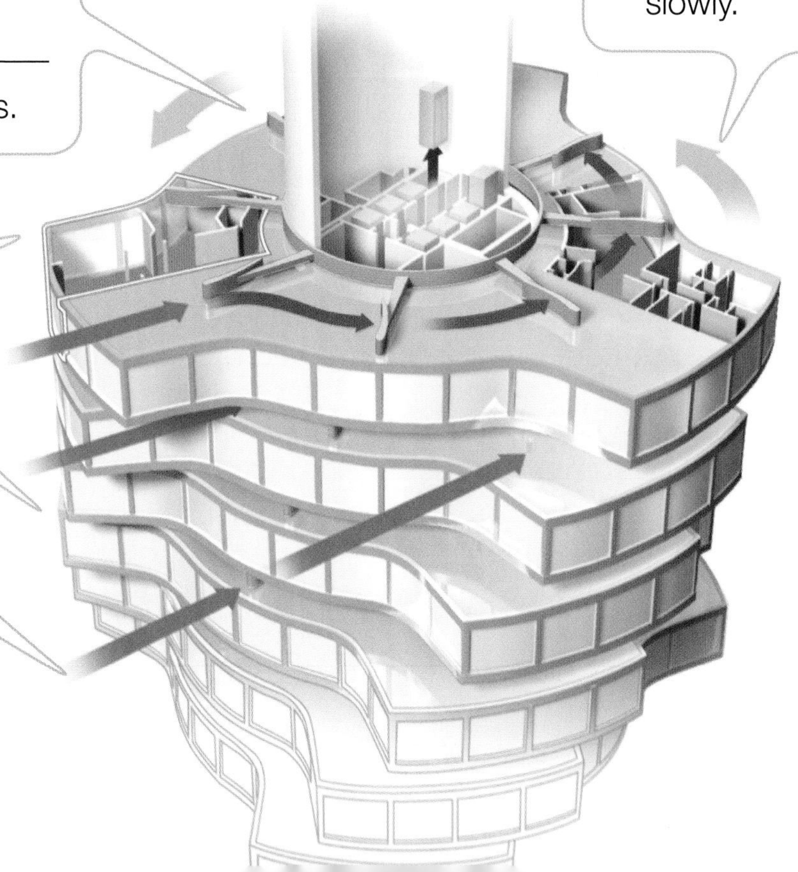

Language Practice

A Vocabulary: Completion. Complete the sentences using a word from the box.

> machines   shape   impossible   sounds
> energy   slowly   humans   speeds

1. Bikes and cars travel at different _____.

2. Before the 1950s, only a few people knew about the _____ we now call computers.

3. The tea was heavy, so the porters carried it up the mountain very _____ .

4. Solar panels can make _____ from the sun.

5. For many people, an architect's job _____ very hard.

6. Some animals can talk a little, but only _____ can use more than one language.

7. For now, living on Mars is still _____.

8. The _____ of most buildings never changes.

Usage

Sound can have two meanings.
(v.) That **sounds** interesting.
Her job **sounds** fun!
(n.) **a loud** sound, **a noisy** sound

B Grammar: Using *however*. Read these sentences.

a. Fisher's ideas sound impossible, **but** that's what people also said before humans traveled into space.

b. Fisher's ideas sound impossible. **However,** that's what people also said before humans traveled into space.

Write a second sentence to finish each idea. Use **however**.

1. The scientists told the people near the volcano to leave their homes.

   _____

2. The Great Pyramid is more than 4,000 years old.

   _____

3. Fisher's building sounds very interesting.

   _____

4. Many people love grizzly bears.

   _____

4B Big Ideas, Small Sizes

◀ This **solar-powered light** is useful for places with no electricity.

The **baby warmer** ▶ is an inexpensive way of keeping babies warm.

The **chili grinder** helps ▶ people grind hot chilies without hurting their hands.

Before You Read

A **Discussion.** Some good designs can help people around the world. Look at the pictures. Why are these inventions good? Talk about your ideas with a partner.

B **Definitions.** Match the words with their meanings.

> **1.** probably   **2.** both   **3.** clean   **4.** roll   **5.** sick   **6.** easy   **7.** last (v.)   **8.** repeat

_____ **a.**

_____ **b.** do again

_____ **c.** not dirty

_____ **d.** When something will _____ happen, it is likely to happen.

_____ **e.**

_____ **f.** two things

_____ **g.** not hard to do

_____ **h.** When things _____, they don't stop or break.

Reading

Strategy: Skimming. Quickly read the passage. Who are these inventions for? Tell a partner.

a. people without clean water

b. people in the U.S.

c. people with a lot of money

Making It Safe

1   Do you drink water every day? Is it clean? You **probably** answered yes to **both** questions. But 900 million people around the world don't have safe drinking water. Without **clean** water, they get **sick** more easily.
5   That's why these two ideas are so great! They can make a big difference for a lot of people.

The LifeStraw

This straw cleans water when you drink through it. It is small and **easy** to carry. You can get clean water
10   anywhere you go. It **lasts** over six months for most people. You don't have to worry about getting a new **one** often.

The Q Drum

This new **container** helps people
15   carry clean water to their homes. In rural places, people often have to walk to get clean water. Then they have to carry it back to their homes. They **repeat** this every
20   time they need water, but water is heavy! You don't have to lift the Q Drum. You can **roll** it home. No more carrying 50 kilograms of water!

Reading Comprehension

A Circle the correct answer.

Detail   **1.** The passage says that 900 million people _____.

     a. need clean water   **b.** use the LifeStraw   **c.** carry water to their homes

Reference   **2.** In line 12, the word **one** refers to _____.

     a. a straw   **b.** a container   **c.** water

Vocabulary   **3.** Which of these is a **container** (line 14)?

     a. a chair   **b.** a box   **c.** a knife

Inference   **4.** The writer probably thinks _____.

     a. carrying water is very easy for most people
     b. the straw is more useful than the container
     c. most people don't really think about their water

B   **Strategy: Classification.** Which invention(s) do these sentences describe. Write **a** to **f** in the correct place.

     a. It helps people have clean water.   **d.** It is heavy, but you can roll it.

     b. You can carry it.   **e.** It helps people take water to their homes.

     c. It's easy to use.   **f.** It helps people not get sick.

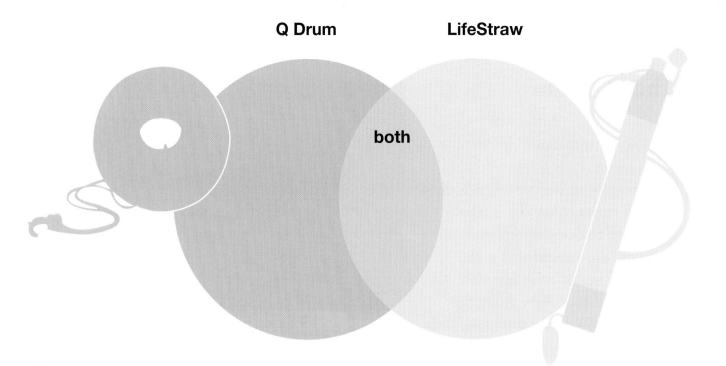

Q Drum   **LifeStraw**

both

Language Practice

A Vocabulary: Words in context. Share your answers with your partner.

1. What are some times when you **repeat** what someone says?

_____

2. What are some things you can **roll**?

_____

3. What do you think is popular now but **probably** won't be popular in a year?

_____

4. What do you do when you are **sick**?

_____

5. What do **both** your mother and father like to do?

_____

6. Do you think studying English is **easy**?

_____

7. Give an example of something that **lasts** more than a year.

_____

8. How often do you **clean** your room?

_____

B Grammar: *have to / don't have to*. Read these sentences from the passage.

a. You **don't have to** worry about getting a new one soon.
b. In rural places, people often **have to** walk to get clean water.
c. Then they **have to** carry it back to their homes.
d. You **don't have to** lift the Q Drum.

Usage

Use ***have to / don't have to*** with *I, you, we,* or *they.*

Use ***has to / doesn't have to*** with *he, she,* or *it.*

Complete each sentence using **have to / don't have to** so they are true for you. Compare answers with a partner.

1. I _____ walk to school every day.

2. I _____ make my own lunch every day.

3. On Sunday, I _____.

4. In my English class, we _____.

 # Video

Solar Cooking

A **Preview.** Look at the pictures and label the different ways of cooking food.

> electricity   gas
> solar energy   wood fire

1 _____

2 _____ 3 _____ 4 _____

B **As you watch.** Choose True (**T**) or False (**F**) for each sentence.

1. Solar cooking is both fast and cheap.   **T**   **F**

2. SCI shows people how to use solar energy.   **T**   **F**

3. When the WAPI's wax melts, people can drink the water.   **T**   **F**

4. Before solar cookers, most of the women in the video cooked using gas.   **T**   **F**

C **Think about it.** How is solar cooking better for the Earth than other ways of cooking?

Vocabulary Review

Words in context. Unscramble the underlined words. Then use them to complete the sentences.

1. We need a <u>h a m i c e n</u> to help us <u>f l i t</u> this <u>v a h e y</u> box.

   We need a _____ to help us _____ this _____ box.

2. My sister loves to <u>l e t v a r</u>. Her next <u>p r i t</u> will <u>p o b b a l r y</u> be to China.

   My sister loves to _____. Her next _____ will _____ be to China.

3. It is <u>y a s e</u> to <u>s c o r s</u> the river <u>u n g r i d</u> the dry season.

   It is _____ to _____ the river _____ the dry season.

4. <u>h o B t</u> soccer <u>m a s t e</u> play games <u>r o n u d a</u> the world.

   _____ soccer _____ play games _____ the world.

5. It was <u>b o s i m i p e l s</u> to <u>l o r l</u> the <u>u g e h</u> rock up the hill.

   It was _____ to _____ the _____ rock up the hill.

World Heritage Notes

Notes Completion. Scan the information on pages 58 and 59 to complete the notes.

What: The Great Wall of China
Where: China
Data:

- It is known to the Chinese people as the *Long Wall of* _____.
- China's first emperor _____ brought together many of the original wall pieces.
- At first, the wall was built of stone, _____, grass, and _____.
- Every year, about _____ tourists visit China's Great Wall.
- The leaders of the Zhou tribe built small walls to protect their land from _____ from the north.
- During the Ming dynasty, the Ming kings also added _____ for guards to watch from and _____ along the wall for soldiers to live in.

The Great Wall of China

Site: **The Great Wall of China**

Location: **China**

Category: **Cultural**

Status: **World Heritage Site since 1987**

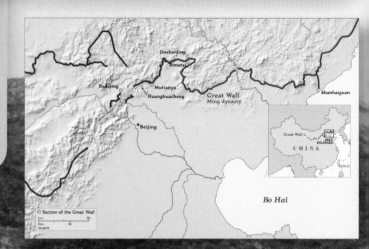

770–476 B.C.

The leaders of the Zhou tribe built small walls along China's northern border to protect their land from warrior[1] tribes from the north. These walls were made of earth and were only two meters high.

[1] A **warrior** is a fighter or soldier. He or she is good at fighting.

475–221 B.C.

At this time, seven different tribes were fighting each other for land and power in China. Each ruler built small walls to protect themselves. Some of the rulers also built more walls to the north, to keep their enemies out of China.

221–207 B.C.

Emperor Qin Shi Huang brought the seven tribes together and became the first emperor of China. He joined up all the small walls that were already built, and also built over 5,000 kilometers (about 3,000 miles) of new wall across the land.

206 B.C.–A.D. 220

The emperors of the Han dynasty[2] worked to make the Great Wall stronger. They also made it longer, so that it went all the way to the edge of the Gobi desert.

[2] A **dynasty** is a line of rulers of a country all from one family.

770–476 B.C.   475–221 B.C.   221–207 B.C.   206 B.C.

The Great Wall of China is famous for being the largest man-made structure in the world. It is known to the Chinese people as the *Long Wall of Ten Thousand Li.* One *li* is about half a kilometer. Many people think the Great Wall of China is just one long wall. But today's Great Wall is really a collection of different sections of wall built in different places.

At first, the wall was built of stone, wood, grass, and earth. In later years, the builders used bricks to make the old walls stronger and make new walls last longer. These pieces of wall were built part by part, by different rulers, over 2,000 years. China's first emperor, Qin Shi Huang, brought together many of the original wall pieces into one wall.

Today, many parts of the wall are gone. About 50 percent of the original ancient structure is not there anymore. But the parts still standing are some of China's most popular tourist sites. Each year, about ten million tourists visit China's Great Wall, making it the world's largest outdoor museum.

A.D. 1368–1644

The emperors of the Ming dynasty rebuilt many parts of the old wall that were falling down. They also made it even longer, more than 6,700 kilometers (4,100 miles) long. The Ming emperors also added towers for guards to watch from and houses along the wall for the soldiers to live in.

−A.D. 220	A.D. 1368–1644	Today

A Chinese Folktale

Meng Chiang-nu and the Great Wall

1   Thousands of years ago, in China, there was an emperor, Shi Huang. He made people from all over China work on the Great Wall. The work was long and hard. Many workers died.

A beautiful woman, Meng Chiang-nu, lived with her husband in a small
5   village. Her husband had to go north to work on the Great Wall. It was very, very cold in the north. He was gone for many months.

One day, Meng Chiang-nu went to find her husband. She walked for days and days. She walked across rivers and mountains. Finally, she reached the Great Wall. "Where is my husband?" she asked.

10   "Oh, he died long ago," a man said. "We buried him here, by the Wall." Meng Chiang-nu cried. She cried for days, and many people cried with her. Their tears made a river 300 meters long. They cried so hard that a part of the wall fell down.

When the emperor heard about the woman, he came to see what had
15   happened. He saw her crying, and fell in love with her. "Will you marry me?" he asked. "I will marry you," Meng Chiang-nu said. "But first, you must build a tomb[1] for my husband." The emperor agreed.

When the tomb was finished, Meng Chiang-nu wouldn't marry the emperor. She jumped into the river. "Catch her! Catch her!" the emperor **shouted**. But
20   Meng Chiang-nu became a beautiful silver fish. She swam away, into the green-blue water.

[1] A **tomb** is a place or building for a dead person.

Reading Comprehension

Circle the correct answer.

Detail   **1.** Why did Meng Chiang-nu travel to the Great Wall of China?
   a. to find her husband
   b. her husband asked her to
   c. to work on the Wall

Inference   **2.** Which word describes Meng Chiang-nu's trip to the Great Wall?
   a. easy   **b.** hard   **c.** impossible

Detail   **3.** What made part of the wall fall down?
   a. the workers' shouting made it fall down
   b. Meng Chiang-nu's crying brought it down
   c. the workers hit it, and made it fall down

Vocabulary   **4.** In line 19, what does **shouted** mean?
   a. said loudly   **b.** said softly   **c.** asked

Vocabulary Extension

A **Vocabulary: Collocation.** Match the verbs on the left with the objects on the right.

   1. carry   ○   ○   **a.** a ball
   2. cross   ○   ○   **b.** a box
   3. cut   ○   ○   **c.** a cake
   4. dig   ○   ○   **d.** a hole
   5. repeat   ○   ○   **e.** a river
   6. roll   ○   ○   **f.** a word

B Complete the sentences using the phrases you made in **A**.

   1. Before you put a new plant in your garden, you need to _____ .
   2. From the top of a hill, you can _____ down to the bottom.
   3. To go from south London to north London, you have to _____ .
   4. You can _____ of books to the library.
   5. Students often have to _____ many times to learn it.
   6. At a birthday party, you usually _____ into several pieces.

Striking It Rich

Treasure from the ship *The Whydah Galley*. The ship sank in a storm in 1717.

Warm Up

Talk with a partner.

1. To *strike it rich* means to be suddenly very lucky. Do you know anyone who has struck it rich?
2. Have you ever found money or something expensive?

Winning the Lottery

a lottery ticket seller in Rangoon, Burma

Before You Read

A Discussion. Have you ever won anything? Tell your partner.

B Definitions. Match the words with their meanings.

> **1.** famous **2.** hide **3.** escape **4.** finally **5.** news **6.** lucky **7.** win **8.** rich

_____ **a.** get away from a place or person you don't like

_____ **b.** When someone has a lot of money, they are _____.

_____ **c.** When someone is _____, many people know about him or her.

_____ **d.** be number one, or come first, in something, e.g. a contest

_____ **e.** information about things that have just happened

_____ **f.** lastly, after a long time

_____ **g.** Someone is _____ when good things happen to them by chance.

_____ **h.** to put something in a place where it is hard to find

▲ Sheelah Ryan (right) meets friends after winning the lottery.

Sheelah Ryan didn't get all her money at one time. The prize was $2,767,361 every year for 20 years. ▲

Reading

Strategy: Predicting. This passage is about a lottery winner. Check (✓) the things you think she did with her money.

 took a trip

 bought more lottery tickets

☐ bought a new house

☐ helped other people

A REAL WINNER

1 Does money make people happy? Some people think so, but read about Sheelah Ryan.

Ryan often bought lottery tickets but wasn't **lucky**. Then, one day, she got some amazing **news**. She **won** $55 million, and she was suddenly **famous**.

5 In that one day, her life changed. People knew she was **rich**, so over 750,000 people wrote letters to her. They were all asking for money. News reporters[1] wanted to talk to her. She couldn't get away from **them**. She **finally** moved to a new house so she could **escape**.

[1] a news reporter

The story doesn't end there, though. Ryan didn't just **hide** from everyone.

10 With the money, she started a group called the Ryan Foundation. The foundation helps students go to college. It also helps women and small children. When they can't pay their rent[2] one month, the foundation helps them pay it.

The foundation is still helping people. Today, Ryan is famous for the good things she did with her money.

[2] **Rent** is money you pay to live in a house.

Reading Comprehension

A Circle the correct answer.

Detail **1.** Who does the Ryan Foundation help with their rent?

    a. lottery winners   **b.** news reporters   **c.** women and children

Purpose **2.** The purpose of the fourth paragraph (from line 9) is to tell us _____.

    a. why Sheelah was unhappy
    b. how Sheelah used her money
    c. where Sheelah went after she won

Main Idea **3.** What could be another title for this passage?

    a. How Lotteries Work
    b. How to Win a Lottery
    c. Using Her Luck to Help People

Detail **4.** What did NOT happen after Sheelah won her money?

    a. Reporters asked her questions.
    b. She moved to another house.
    c. She wrote a lot of letters.

B **Strategy: Sequencing.** Number the events in order from **1** to **5**.

    a. _____ Sheelah bought lottery tickets and won.

    b. _____ People wanted money from Sheelah.

    c. _____ Sheelah started the Ryan Foundation.

    d. _____ Sheelah bought lottery tickets but didn't win.

    e. _____ Sheelah became famous for doing good things.

Some lotteries use balls to
choose winning numbers.

> ## Word Partners
>
> **Use *luck* with:**
> (*adj.*) **good** luck, **bad** luck
> (*v.*) **bring someone** luck, **need a little/some** luck,
> **wish *someone*** luck, **have good/bad** luck

Language Practice

A **Vocabulary: Words in context.** Circle the best answer.

1. Parents often _____ a present[1] before their child's birthday.
   a. hide   **b.** lift

2. Rich people _____.
   a. can buy a lot of things   **b.** don't have much money

3. You can read news _____.
   a. in a book   **b.** on the Internet

4. Which of these do people sometimes want to escape from?
   a. a tiger   **b.** a lottery

5. When you buy a lottery ticket, you want to be _____ .
   a. lucky   **b.** cut

6. The pyramids in Egypt are _____ around the world.
   a. final   **b.** famous

7. Most sports teams want to _____.
   a. win   **b.** escape

8. When something finally happens, it happens after a _____ time.
   a. long   **b.** very short

[1] **a present**

B **Grammar: Past continuous.** Read these sentences.

> **a.** They **were** all **asking** for money.
>
> **b.** As the reporters **were walking** down the mountain, the volcano started to erupt.

The sentences below all have mistakes. Write the sentences, correcting the mistakes.

1. Ian's dad is taking pictures when he saw an elephant.

   _____

2. The porters was carrying tea when it started to snow.

   _____

3. The workers were putting a block into the pyramid every three minutes.

   _____

4. Mount Merapi was smoking, so all of the people were leaving their homes.

   _____

5B Fantastic Finds

▲ Two treasure hunters in Mexico show a plate from a sunken ship.

Before You Read

A Discussion. Do you have anything very old? Is it worth a lot of money? Talk with your partner.

B Definitions. Match the words with their meanings.

> **1.** find out **2.** worth **3.** expert **4.** plan
> **5.** laugh **6.** special **7.** sell **8.** item

_____ **a.** have an idea to do something

_____ **b.** what you do when something is funny

_____ **c.** learn, discover something

_____ **d.** a person knowing a lot about something

_____ **e.** let someone have something for money

_____ **f.** one thing

_____ **g.** important to a person

_____ **h.** how much money something can be sold for

Reading

Strategy: Scanning. What is the name of the ship the menu is from?

_____

Read and check your answer.

Old But VALUABLE

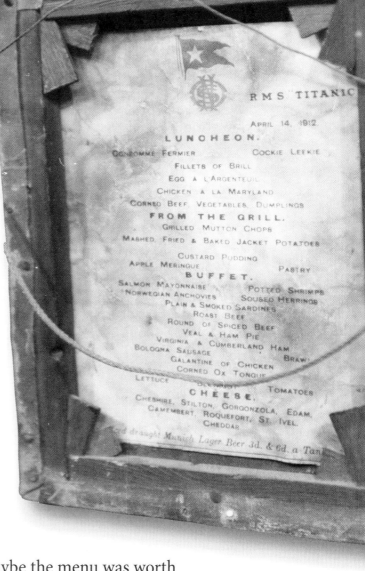

1 The next time you find something unusual, look again. Maybe it's worth more than you think!

Look closely at this menu. Why do you
5 think it is **special**? This menu is from the famous ship, the *Titanic*. It's from the *Titanic*'s final lunch before it sank. In 1971, the menu was on the back of a $45 painting. Fred Kelly bought the painting
10 and menu. He didn't think about it very much. Then in 1998, the movie *Titanic* became very popular. Fred's wife thought maybe the menu was worth up to $5,000. They took it to an **expert**—and **found out** it was **worth** $65,000! She **laughed**.

Star Wars action figures

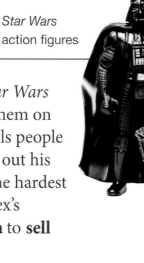

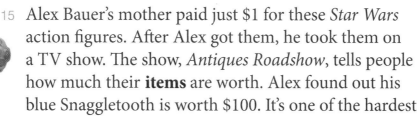

15 Alex Bauer's mother paid just $1 for these *Star Wars* action figures. After Alex got them, he took them on a TV show. The show, *Antiques Roadshow*, tells people how much their **items** are worth. Alex found out his blue Snaggletooth is worth $100. It's one of the hardest
20 *Star Wars* action figures to find. Together, Alex's figures are worth $250–$300! He doesn't **plan** to **sell them**, at least not right now.

Reading Comprehension

A Circle the correct answer.

Inference **1.** What was NOT true about the painting?

    a. It had a menu on the back.   **b.** Fred Kelly painted it.   **c.** Fred bought it in 1971.

Detail **2.** Who thought the menu was worth up to $5,000 in 1998?

    a. Fred   **b.** Fred's wife   **c.** an expert

Reference **3.** On line 22, the word **them** refers to the _____ .

    a. TV shows   **b.** people on the show   **c.** action figures

Detail **4.** The blue Snaggletooth is worth more than other figures because it _____ .

    a. was on a TV show   **b.** is very big   **c.** is difficult to find

B **Strategy: Classification.** Which item(s) do these sentences describe? Write **a** to **e** in the correct place.

It was/They were _____ .

    a. worth more than the buyer thought
    b. worth thousands of dollars
    c. more than 50 years old.
    d. a present from someone
    e. on TV

action figures

Titanic menu

both

Language Practice

A Vocabulary: Completion. Use your own ideas. Share your answers with a partner.

1. I **plan to** _____ next year.

2. My _____ always **laughs** when _____.

3. Right now, I don't want to **sell** my _____.

4. _____ is **worth** _____.

5. The best way to **find out** something is _____.

6. I think _____ is **special**.

7. The oldest **item** I own is _____.

8. I'm not an **expert**, but I know a lot about _____.

B Grammar: Joining clauses. Read these sentences; **a** is from the passage.

a. They took it to an expert—and found out it was worth $65,000!

b. This was the volcano Arne went into—and now it was our turn to go inside!

c. These men and women—called porters—carried tea on their backs.

Rewrite the two sentences as one sentence. Use dashes (—).
Then write two sentences with your own ideas. Use dashes (—).

1. Suddenly, the building moved. And the shape changed.

_____

2. The volcano erupted last year. It is called Mount Merapi.

_____

3. _____

4. _____

Word Partners

Use _worth_ with:
(*n.*) worth **five dollars**, worth **money**, worth the **trouble**, worth **a try**
(*v.*) worth **buying**, worth **having**, worth **remembering**, worth **doing**

Treasure Under My Home

old Egyptian artifacts ▶

▲ a tomb in Egypt

A Preview. You will hear these words in the video. Match each word to its definition.

> **a.** artifact **b.** illegal **c.** incredible **d.** secret **e.** smuggle **f.** tunnel

_____ **1.** not allowed by law or the police

_____ **2.** amazing

_____ **3.** not told to anyone

_____ **4.** a long hole in the ground from one place to another

_____ **5.** to illegally take things from one country to another

_____ **6.** an old and culturally interesting item

B After you watch. Watch the video, then circle true (**T**) or false (**F**) for each sentence.

1. Smugglers sell artifacts illegally.	T	F
2. Dr. Hiebert used to be a smuggler.	T	F
3. Some people in Egypt find artifacts under their homes.	T	F
4. Most of these artifacts are very cheap to buy.	T	F
5. The police are trying to teach people about their history.	T	F
6. Lisa Ling saw artifacts worth $30,000.	T	F

C Think about it. Do you think it's OK to sell treasure you find under your house? Talk with a partner.

Killer Plants

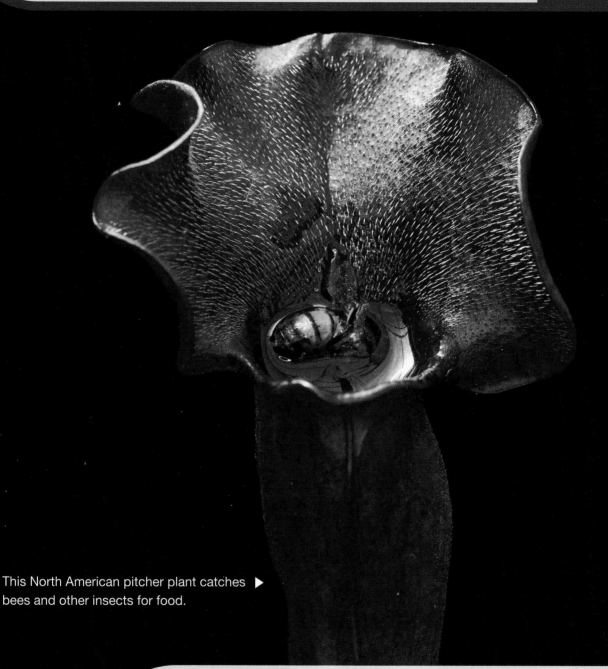

This North American pitcher plant catches ▶
bees and other insects for food.

Warm Up

Talk with a partner.

1. Can plants eat? Do they drink?
2. Do you know the names of any famous scientists?
   Who are they?

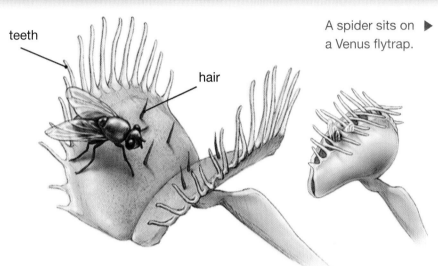

teeth

hair

A spider sits on ▶
a Venus flytrap.

The Venus flytrap is **carnivorous**
(it eats meat). There are over 675 kinds
of carnivorous plants in the world.

Before You Read

A Quiz. What do you know about carnivorous plants? Circle **True** or **False** for
the sentences below. Then check your answers at the bottom of the page.

1. Carnivorous plants eat insects.	**True**	**False**
2. Carnivorous plants only live in hot places.	**True**	**False**
3. All carnivorous plants have "teeth" to catch food.	**True**	**False**

B Definitions. Match the words with their meanings.

> **1.** die   **2.** fall   **3.** ready   **4.** close (*v.*)   **5.** touch   **6.** cover (*v.*)   **7.** land (*v.*)   **8.** nice

_____ **a.** to feel

_____ **b.** the opposite of *open*

_____ **c.** OK to do something now

_____ **d.** to stop on the ground
after flying

_____ **e.** put something on top of another thing

_____ **f.** good

_____ **g.** suddenly move down from a high place

_____ **h.** to stop living

1. T 2. F Carnivorous plants live around the world. 3. F. Venus flytraps
have teeth, but plants like sundews and pitcher plants do not.

Reading

Strategy: Scanning. How many ways of catching insects does the passage talk about?

Plants That Eat Insects

A Venus flytrap catches a fly in its teeth.

1 The next time you see an insect on a plant, watch closely. It may be that plant's lunch![1]

A fly lands on a Venus flytrap. It **touches**
5 the flytrap's very small hairs twice. In less than a second, the flytrap **closes**. There is no time for the fly to escape. After the flytrap closes, the teeth make a cage.[2] The flytrap slowly eats the insect over the next
10 10 days. Then it opens again. It's **ready** to catch its next meal!

An insect wants something to drink. It **lands** on this beautiful Australian sundew. The "water" sticks to the insect, and **it**
15 can't escape. Slowly, the plant **covers** the insect with a liquid. The **bug** slowly **dies**.

A small insect is stuck on a sundew.

What's that **nice** smell? Insects like the smell, too, so they land on this pitcher plant. It's slippery,[3] and the bugs **fall** in.
20 The inside of the pitcher plant is slippery, so the insects cannot climb out. Slowly, the plant kills them.

Dead flies have fallen into a pitcher plant.

[1] **Lunch** is the food you eat in the middle of the day.

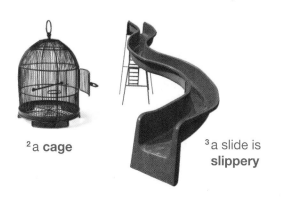

[2] a **cage**

[3] a slide is **slippery**

Reading Comprehension

A Circle the correct answer.

Gist   **1.** The reading is mainly about _____.

     a. insects eating plants   **b.** insects eating bugs   **c.** plants eating insects

Reference   **2.** In line 14, the word **it** refers to the _____.

     a. water   **b.** sundew   **c.** insect

Vocabulary   **3.** We can change **bug** (line 16) with _____.

     a. sundew   **b.** insect   **c.** plant

Sequence   **4.** Which of the following happens first?

     a. The flytrap eats the bug.

     b. The flytrap makes a cage.

     c. The insect touches the flytrap's hairs.

B   **Strategy: Classification.** According to the article, which plant(s) do these sentences describe?

a. It eats bugs.

b. Insects think they can get a drink from it.

c. Bugs land on it because of its smell.

d. It is sticky.

e. Insects can't escape from it.

f. It closes to catch insects.

g. It is slippery.

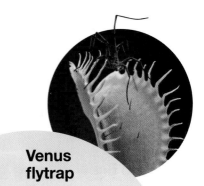

Venus flytrap

sundew

pitcher plant

Language Practice

A Vocabulary: Words in context. Circle the correct answers.

1. Children often _____ off their bikes[1] when they are young.
   a. touch   **b. fall**

2. When you say "That looks **nice** on you,"
   you say someone looks _____.
   a. good   **b.** bad

[1]a **bike**

3. Which of these do you usually use to **touch** something?
   a. your finger   **b.** water

4. Which of these can you **close**?
   a. a door[2]   **b.** an insect

5. Which of these **lands** at the end of a trip?
   a. an airplane   **b.** a car

[2]a **door**

6. Which of these can **die**?
   a. a bird   **b.** a rock

7. "I'm **ready**" means "I _____ go now."
   a. can   **b.** can't

Usage

Close can have two meanings:
1. (v.) /klōz/ the opposite of
open, e.g. *Close the door!*
2. (prep.) /klōs/ near, e.g. *My
house is close to my school.*

8. Which of these do you **cover** most often?
   a. a pot   **b.** an airplane

B Grammar: Describing a sequence. Read these sentences;
b is from the passage.

> **a.** The flytrap closes. **Then** the teeth make a cage.
>
> **b. After** the flytrap closes, the teeth make a cage.

Rewrite the two sentences using **after**. Then write two more sentences
with your own ideas.

1. The flytrap eats the insect. Then it opens again.

_____

2. The workers finished one pyramid. Then they started another.

_____

3. _____

4. _____

▲ A sundew catches a fly.

Before You Read

A **Discussion.** What do you know about Charles Darwin? Tell a partner.

B **Definitions.** Match the words with their meanings.

Charles Darwin ▶ was a British scientist. He lived from 1809 to 1882. He studied plants and animals, and did many **experiments**.[1]

Ch. Darwin
March 7th 1874.

1. body	**2.** carefully	**3.** center
4. decide	**5.** examine	**6.** later
7. several	**8.** toward	

_____ **a.** the middle

_____ **b.** the whole person or animal, with arms, legs, and head

_____ **c.** at a time after

_____ **d.** to, in the direction of

_____ **e.** to look at a lot, to study

_____ **f.** a few, more than two

_____ **g.** to choose

_____ **h.** slowly and with no mistakes

[1] An **experiment** is a scientific test to find out something.

Reading

Strategy: Skimming. The reading is about some of Charles Darwin's experiments. Was he mainly interested in insects or plants? Tell a partner.

Darwin's Diary

1 Can plants kill flies? In the summer, I found sundew plants with many insects on them. I decided to examine them more carefully. I examined 12 plants, and I found 31 dead insects, or parts of their bodies.

5 Some leaves caught several insects. The sundew plant catches flies much more often than other insects. I want to do some experiments. I don't know what I'll find out.

Experiment 1

10 I put several items in the center of each leaf. The "tentacles" always moved toward the items. The speed was not always the same. Why?

Experiment 2

I found a leaf with a fly on it. The fly could not
15 escape. The fly was on one side of the leaf. The tentacles on that side closed around the fly and killed it. The tentacles from the other side of the leaf never moved!

Experiment 3

20 I put a dead fly in the center of a leaf. The next morning, the leaf was closed. It opened again five days later. There was

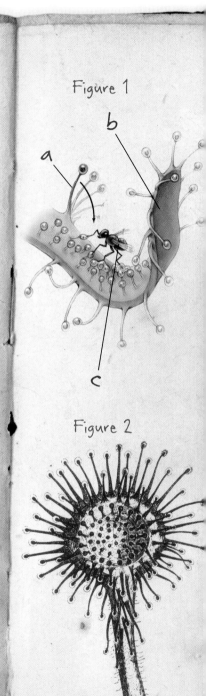

Figure 1

Figure 2

Reading Comprehension

A Circle the correct answer.

Detail **1.** What did Darwin learn?

    a. Sundews can move to catch insects.

    b. Sundews can finish eating an insect in one day.

    c. Sundew tentacles all move at the same speed.

Vocabulary **2.** In this drawing from the diary, the plant's "tentacles" are _____.

    a. a   **b.** b   **c.** c

Inference **3.** How many whole insects did Darwin find on the 12 plants?

    a. fewer than 31   **b.** 31   **c.** more than 31

Prediction **4.** On the next page of the diary, we can probably read "[*There was*] _____."

    a. no fly   **b.** a dead fly   **c.** a living fly

B **Strategy: Summary completion.** Complete the summary using words from the passage.

Charles Darwin looked at 12 (**1**) _____ plants, and found many (**2**) _____ bugs. After this, he decided to do (**3**) _____ different experiments.

In Experiment 1, he put items in the middle of a (**4**) _____. He found that the tentacles moved (**5**) _____. But the tentacles didn't all move at the same (**6**) _____. In Experiment 2, he found a leaf with (**7**) _____ on it. He saw that the tentacles near the bug (**8**) _____ it, but the ones on the other side (**9**) _____.

In the last experiment, he put (**10**) _____ on a leaf. A day later, he saw the leaf was (**11**) _____. Then five days later it (**12**) _____.

sundews in Europe ▶

Language Practice

A Vocabulary: Words in context. Circle the best word in each sentence.

¹a donut

1. *Later* means (**before** / **after**) a time.

2. Donuts¹ have a hole in their (**center** / **body**).

3. Doctors² (**examine** / **decide**) sick people.

4. Some people have several (**legs** / **brothers**).

5. Nurses³ (**have** / **don't have**) to be careful in their work.

6. When you get a pet cat, you need to (**examine** / **decide**) what its name will be.

7. A person's (**center** / **body**) temperature is usually 37°C (98°F).

²a doctor

8. Many bugs fly (**toward** / **from**) light.

B Grammar: Making predictions. Read these sentences; **a** is from the passage.

> **a.** I don't know what I**'ll** find out.
>
> **b.** There **will** be more cars in the future.

³a nurse

Complete the sentences with your ideas. Then write two more sentences with your own ideas. Compare answers with a partner.

1. Six months from now, I'll _____.

2. In 10 years, people around the world will probably _____.

   _____.

3. In 100 years, people _____.

   _____.

4. _____.

5. _____.

Word Link

-ful = filled with
beauti**ful**, color**ful**, care**ful**

Video

Plants

a toucan in Peru ▶
eating fruit

fruit

A **Preview.** How do plants and animals help each other? Do you know any interesting plants? Make a list.

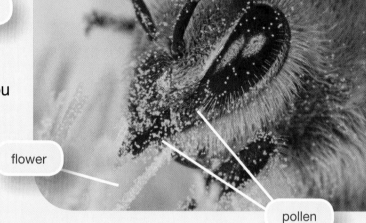

flower

pollen

▲ pollen on a bee's face

B **After you watch.** Match each animal to a statement.

  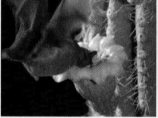 

1. _____ 2. _____ 3. _____ 4. _____

a. It eats the fruit so the seed falls.

b. It's food for the plant.

c. It eats smaller animals.

d. It takes pollen to other flowers.

C **Think about it.** Are there other ways animals and plants need each other?

Vocabulary Review

Opposites. Match the words with their opposites.

1. hide   ○   ○   **a.** away
2. win   ○   ○   **b.** buy
3. rich   ○   ○   **c.** catch
4. laugh   ○   ○   **d.** cry
5. sell   ○   ○   **e.** live
6. die   ○   ○   **f.** lose
7. close   ○   ○   **g.** open
8. toward   ○   ○   **h.** poor
9. escape   ○   ○   **i.** show

World Heritage Notes

Notes Completion. Scan the information on pages 84 and 85 to complete the notes.

What: Central Amazon
Conservation Complex

Where: _____

Data:

- The _____ _____ is the biggest
  river in the world.

- The Amazon rain forest makes _____ of the world's oxygen.

- _____ otters and poison _____
  frogs live there.

- There are _____ of different kinds of plants and
  animals in the Amazon rain forest.

- Many of the animals and plants in the Amazon are
  _____.

Central Amazon

Site: **Central Amazon Conservation Complex**

Location: **South America**

Category: **Natural**

Status: **World Heritage Site since 2000**

The Amazon rain forest is the largest rain forest in the world. More than half of all the rain forests left on Earth are there. The area covers about two thirds of the South American continent. It covers parts of nine different countries, including Brazil, Colombia, and Peru. This big forest makes up to 20% of the world's oxygen for us to breathe.

The Amazon rain forest is a place of giant things. The jaguar—the biggest of the American big cats—and the largest otter live in the Amazon. The mighty Amazon River runs through the forest. It is the largest river on Earth. The water from the river helps millions of kinds of plants and animals to live and grow. Many of these animals and plants are endangered.

The Central Amazon Conservation[1] Complex[2] lies between two big rivers in South America—the Amazon River and the Río Negro (Black River). It covers over 60,000 square kilometers (6 million hectares) of the Amazon rain forest. People cannot cut down trees or kill animals in the complex, so the plants and the animals that live there are safe.

Beautiful flowers and plants like these orchids add bright colors to the rainforest. There are thousands of different orchid species in the Amazon.

[1] **conservation:** the protection of nature and animals
[2] **complex:** a place with many different parts

The giant otter

The giant otter lives in the forests near the Amazon River. Adult giant otters can grow up to 1.8 meters (6 feet) long. They swim very well, and catch all the fish they eat from the river. Giant otters live in big families with their parents, brothers, and sisters. Some people kill these otters for their fur. Also, a lot of the forest they live in is gone. So there are only a few thousand giant otters left in the Amazon.

The jaguar

Today, jaguars are only found in the rain forests of Central and South America. An adult jaguar can weigh more than 140 kilograms (300 pounds) and grow to more than two meters (eight feet) long from nose to tail. In most countries in the Amazon, the law says you cannot hunt jaguars. But some people still do, so the jaguars are still in trouble.

The poison dart frog

The poison dart frog is one of the most interesting, and most dangerous, species in the Amazon. The frog's skin has a dangerous poison that can hurt other animals when they try to eat it. While many other frog species use their brown or green skin to hide in the forest, the poison dart frog uses its bright colors to tell animals: "I'm dangerous! Don't eat me!" The poison dart frog is an animal in trouble because people are cutting down the trees it lives in.

A BRAZILIAN FOLKTALE
THE CURUPIRA

1   For many centuries, the people of the Amazon Basin[1] have told stories about the curupira. Some say the curupira is a boy. Others say it is a girl. However, everyone agrees that it is small, and it has wild red hair, and big pointed ears. A curupira has very special feet; its feet point backwards! Many people in Brazil

5   believe the curupira looks after all the plants and animals in the forest. Any hunter can kill enough to feed his family, but no more. That is the curupira's rule.

  Once upon a time, there lived a hunter called Carlos. Carlos wanted to catch animals for his family to eat, but he was unlucky. He could not catch any animals. Finally, he decided to ask the curupira for help. Everyone knows the curupira

10   likes gifts. Carlos left honey under a tree for the curupira. Suddenly, Carlos was very lucky. That day, he killed two birds. Carlos's family had lots to eat.

  One day, a man said to Carlos, "How many animals can you kill for me? I will pay you lots of money." Carlos thought this was a good idea. He went into the forest, and hunted for several days. He killed many animals: birds, and pigs,

15   and deer.

  Suddenly, a chicken without feathers walked out of the forest.

  "What are you doing?" it asked. Carlos heard a voice from the forest say: "Estefan! Are my animals there?" It was the curupira! "Yes, Curupira, they are all here!" the chicken replied.

20   "Then bring them here!" Curupira said. The chicken touched each dead animal and said, "Wake up! Curupira wants you!" The animals all got up and walked away, into the forest. Carlos was very scared. He wanted to hide. The curupira said to the chicken, "Let him escape." Carlos ran from the forest, and never made the curupira angry again.

[1] **The Amazon Basin** is the part of South America around the Amazon River.

Reading Comprehension

Circle the correct answer.

Detail **1.** The curupira has _____ hair and _____ feet.
  a. black, small
  b. red, special
  c. brown, big

Vocabulary **2.** The curupira has *pointed* ears. What shape is *pointed*?

  a.   **b.** **c.**

Detail **3.** What does the curupira look after?
  a. hunters and their families
  b. plants and animals of the forest
  c. honey and chickens without feathers

Purpose **4.** Why did Carlos kill many animals and birds?
  a. to get money
  b. to feed his family
  c. to give gifts to the curupira

Sequence **5.** In the story, which of the following happens first?
  a. The chicken talks to the animals.
  b. Curupira talks to the chicken.
  c. The chicken talks to Curupira.

Vocabulary Extension

Vocabulary: Prepositions. Circle the best preposition to complete
each sentence.

1. The people (**for** / **of** / **on**) the Amazon Basin have told stories about the curupira for many years.

2. Carlos left gifts for the curupira (**near** / **on** / **under**) a tree.

3. The man wanted to pay Carlos money (**for** / **to** / **with**) the animals he killed.

4. A chicken without feathers came (**inside** / **into** / **out of**) the forest.

5. Carlos was scared. He ran away (**from** / **of** / **with**) the curupira.

The Night Sky

A starry sky over ▲
Owachomo Bridge,
Natural Bridges National
Monument, Utah, U.S.A.
This area is the United
States' first Dark Sky Park.

Warm Up

Talk with a partner.

1. Where is a good place to see stars?
2. Which stars or planets can you name?

7A Light Pollution

Before You Read

▲ **Light pollution** from Chicago lights clouds in the night sky.

A **Discussion.** In cities, there are many electric lights. At night, the light doesn't only shine down. The light often escapes into the night sky. This is called light pollution. Try to answer these questions with a partner.

1. Why do you think light pollution is a problem?

2. What can people do about light pollution?

B **Definitions.** Match the words with their meanings.

> **1.** health   **2.** effect (*n.*)   **3.** affect (*v.*)   **4.** ground (*n.*)
>
> **5.** save   **6.** positive   **7.** fill (*v.*)   **8.** focus (*v.*)

_____ **a.** to make something change

_____ **b.** the part of the Earth under your feet

_____ **c.** keep

_____ **d.** to put as much as you can into a container

_____ **e.** how well your body or mind is

_____ **f.** something that changes because of something else

_____ **g.** to turn something so it clearly goes in one direction, e.g. light into a camera

_____ **h.** good; +

▲ Electric lights fill the night sky of Los Angeles, U.S.A., with light.

Reading

Strategy: Scanning. When did light pollution become a problem? _____

The End of Night

1 Look up at the sky at night. What can you see? Before electric lights, people could often see about 2,500 different stars. Now, light **fills** the skies over our cities. **This** is called light pollution. Because of it, people in cities can often only see about ten stars!

Most of the time, light helps us. We can see because of it. It gives plants energy. But light
5 isn't always good. We need times of dark to rest. One hundred years ago, we had those times of dark. Now the night is like day. Some scientists are worried about how this light **affects** our **health**. These scientists are studying the **effects** of light pollution.

Other scientists are finding ways to stop light pollution and make our lives better. For example, many streetlights now have covers. The covers **focus** the light toward
10 the **ground**. They stop the light from going up into the sky. They also **save** energy. The covers are a small change, but they can still have a **positive** effect.

◀ Covered streetlights save the night sky in Florida, U.S.A.

Reading Comprehension

A Circle the correct answer.

Detail   **1.** Which of these effects of light pollution is NOT talked about in the passage?

    a. It can be bad for people's health.

    b. It stops people from seeing the night sky.

    c. It hurts birds and other animals.

Reference   **2.** In line 2, the word **this** refers to _____ .

    a. light from stars   **b.** electric light   **c.** daylight

Detail   **3.** How many good effects from street light covers does the passage talk about?

    a. one   **b.** two   **c.** three

Inference   **4.** Which statement does the author probably agree with?

    a. People should use fewer lights.

    b. Only big changes are important.

    c. Scientists worry too much about this problem.

B **Strategy: Identifying main and supporting ideas.** Match the ideas below to the correct paragraph. Is each idea a main idea or a supporting idea? Write **a** to **f** in the table.

a. Electric lights cause light pollution.

b. Light gives plants energy.

c. Scientists are finding ways to stop light pollution.

d. People in cities can only see about ten stars.

e. Light has good and bad effects.

f. Streetlight covers focus light toward the ground.

Paragraph	1	2	3
Main Idea			
Supporting Idea			

In some places, like ▶ here in Burkina Faso, people can still see about 2,500 stars.

Language Practice

A Vocabulary: Words in context. Answer the questions below.

1. What is one **effect** of going to bed late every night?

   _____

2. What is one **positive** effect of studying English?

   _____

3. Light pollution is a problem for people in cities. What other kinds of pollution can **affect** people?

   _____

4. How often do you worry about your **health**?

   _____

5. Which do you like better, night or day? Why?

   _____

6. What are three things you can **fill**?

   _____

7. The passage talks about *saving energy*. What other things can you **save**?

   _____

8. You can **focus** light, and you can focus a camera. What else can you focus?

   _____

B Grammar: Using *affect* and *effect*. Read these sentences from the passage.

> **a.** Some scientists are worried about how this light **affects** our health.
>
> **b.** These scientists are studying the **effects** of light pollution.

Choose **affect** or **effect** to complete these sentences.

1. Light pollution has a big (**affect** / **effect**) on night-flying birds.
2. A volcanic eruption near a city will (**affect** / **effect**) people in that city.
3. Many people only worry about what (**affects** / **effects**) them.
4. Scientists don't yet know all the (**affects** / **effects**) of light pollution.

> **Word Partners**
>
> Use *save* with:
> save **money**, save **someone's life**, save **lives**,
> save **time**, save **the world**, save **energy**

Our Solar System

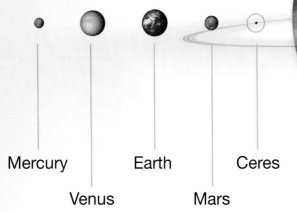

Mercury   Earth   Ceres

Venus   Mars   Jupiter

the Sun

Before You Read

A **Discussion.** How many of the planets above do you know?
Talk about what you know with your partner.

B **Definitions.** Match the words with their meanings.

> **1.** hit (*v.*)   **2.** area   **3.** create   **4.** steep
> **5.** flat   **6.** similar   **7.** wide   **8.** throw

▲ [1] an **asteroid**

____ **a.**

____ **e.** make

____ **b.** almost the same

____ **f.** far from one side to the other

____ **c.** a place

____ **g.**

____ **d.**

____ **h.**

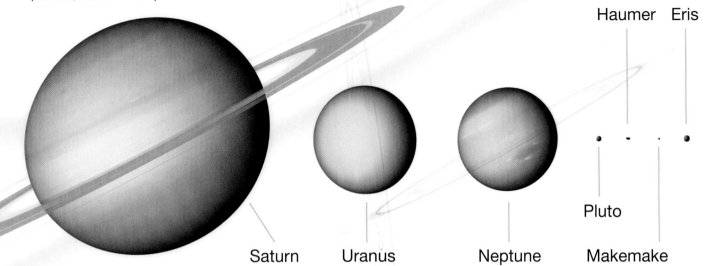

Some astronomers now say the Solar System has 13 planets. These include very small planets, called dwarf planets.

Haumer   Eris

Pluto

Saturn   Uranus   Neptune   Makemake

Reading

Strategy: Identifying the topic. Quickly read the passage. Write each heading in the best place below.

| Craters | Canyons | Volcanoes |

Earth's Neighbor

the planet Mars ▲

1 Mars is about half the size of Earth. In some ways, Mars is **similar** to our planet. However, there are also many differences.

_____

5 As on Earth, there are mountains on Mars. However, they are much larger than Earth's mountains. One of **them** is the largest volcano in the Solar System. It is three times as high as Mount Everest. Unlike Mount Everest, its sides aren't **steep**. It's also **flat** on the top.

_____

Mars also has rocky canyons, just like Earth. They are much larger than Earth's. One of the
10 canyons is 4,000 km long and 200 km **wide**. It is amazing to see!

_____

Sometimes asteroids[1] hit planets. When this happens, they **create** craters. This happens to Earth, too. But asteroids hit Mars much more often than they hit Earth. Scientists think that an asteroid larger than Pluto **hit** Mars. When **this** happened, it **threw** dirt into the air.
15 That dirt covered an **area** as big as the United States!

Reading Comprehension

A Circle the correct answer.

Detail **1.** What is the main purpose of the passage?

      a. to give information about Mars
      b. to show how people might live on Mars
      c. to describe the planets of the Solar System

Reference **2.** In line 6, **them** refers to mountains on _____.

      a. Mars   **b.** Earth   **c.** Mars and Earth

Detail **3.** The biggest volcano on Mars is _____ Mount Everest.

      a. smaller than   **b.** about the same as   **c.** larger than

Reference **4.** In line 14, **this** refers to _____.

      a. Pluto hitting Mars   **b.** an asteroid hitting Mars   **c.** an asteroid hitting Pluto

B **Strategy: Classification.** Which planet(s) do these sentences describe? Write **a** to **f** in the correct place.

  a. It has mountains.

  b. It has the largest volcano in the Solar System.

  c. Its largest mountain is Mount Everest.

  d. It has a canyon 4,000 km long.

  e. Asteroids sometimes hit it.

  f. An asteroid larger than Pluto once hit it.

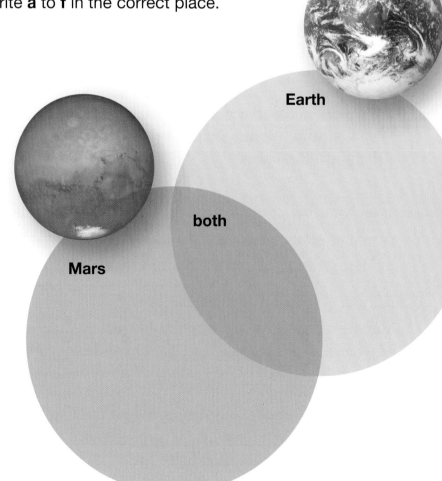

Earth

Mars

both

Language Practice

A **Vocabulary: Words in context.** Choose the best answers for the questions below.

1. Which of these do humans **create**?   **a.** machines   **b.** plants

2. Which of these are more **similar**?   **a.** lions and tigers   **b.** fish and birds

3. Which country has the larger **area**?   **a.** England   **b.** Russia

4. Which of these is **steep**?   **a.** a mountain   **b.** the sea

5. Which of these is **flat**?   **a.** frogs[1]   **b.** tables

[1] a **frog**

6. Which of these can you **throw**?   **a.** cars   **b.** rocks

7. Which of these do people usually **hit**?   **a.** balls   **b.** televisions

8. The Amazon River is up to _____ km **wide**.   **a.** 80   **b.** 6,800

B **Grammar: Comparing things.** Read these sentences; **b** is from the passage.

> **a.** They are much **larger than** Earth's mountains.
>
> **b.** One of them is the **largest** volcano in the Solar System.

Complete the sentences with information about your city, area, or country.

1. The largest _____ is_____.

2. The widest _____ is _____.

3. The longest _____ is _____.

4. _____ is bigger than _____.

5. _____ is steeper than _____.

6. _____ is taller than _____.

Word Partners

Use *steep* with:
steep **hill**, steep **slope**, steep **prices**, steep **increase**

Video

The Solar System

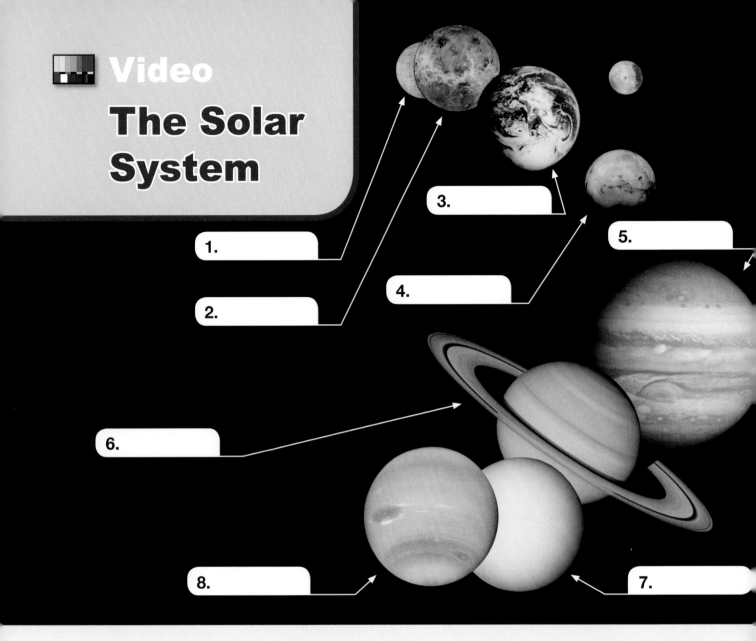

1.

2.

3.

4.

5.

6.

7.

8.

A   Preview. Look at the illustration of the Solar System above and look at the illustration on pages 94 and 95. Write the name of each planet. Then watch the video and check your answers.

B   After you watch. Match the sentences to the correct planet.

1. _____ It's the same size as Earth.   **a.** Jupiter
2. _____ More than 70% of it is water.   **b.** Neptune
3. _____ Its red spot is twice as wide as Earth.   **c.** Venus
4. _____ It has at least 27 moons.   **d.** Uranus
5. _____ It is the windiest place in the Solar System.   **e.** Earth

C   Think about it. Which planet is the most interesting? Why do you think that?

The Olympics

▲ A luge racer practicing at the Winter Olympic Games.

Warm Up

Talk with a partner.

1. What do you know about the Olympics?
2. Who are some famous athletes from your country?

8A The Modern Olympics

Before each Olympic Games, there is a torch relay, a long run with many runners. Each runner carries a torch. The last runner in the relay uses the torch to light the Olympic flame in the stadium. The 2008 Beijing Olympics torch relay had more than 22,000 runners, and went through 21 countries in 138 days.

Olympic flame

stadium

torch

runner

Before You Read

A **Discussion.** Read the paragraph above, and look at the map. Where did the 2008 torch relay start? Where did it finish? Did it go near your country?

▲ The Beijing Olympics Torch Relay. After leaving Ho Chi Minh City, the torch visited more than 100 cities in China.

B **Definitions.** Match the words with their meanings.

| 1. official (n.) | 2. record (n.) | 3. remove | 4. athlete |
| 5. instead of | 6. contain | 7. compete | 8. return |

_____ **a.** someone very good at sports

_____ **b.** e.g. the fastest speed, the highest jump, etc.

_____ **c.** have; include

_____ **d.** to join a sporting event

_____ **e.** a person helping at the Olympics, or other events

_____ **f.** come back; take something back

_____ **g.** to take away; to take out

_____ **h.** rather than; one thing and not another

Reading

Strategy: Scanning. Quickly read the blog below. Which Olympic sport does the writer talk about?

An Olympic Blog

1 ### The Olympic Torch

Every Olympics has a torch relay. The Beijing relay set a new **record**. It was the longest ever. One of my dad's friends ran in the relay. He told

5 me **something** I didn't know. After each runner finishes, Olympic **officials** take the torch and **remove** the gas container. Then they **return** the torch to the runner. This way, the runners can keep their torches. But they can't relight them.

▲ David, the writer of this blog, holds an Olympic torch.

10 ### What You See and What I Saw

When you watch the Olympics on TV, you can see cameras. However, you can't see all of them. Look at the camera in this photo. It moves along a **rail**. It's used to film **athletes** running around the track.

15 ### Athlete Badges

My mom took me to a party. At the party, I met Gabe Gardner. He's on the men's volleyball team. He told me that all the athletes have badges. These

20 badges[1] **contain** computer chips. When officials put Gabe's badge in a computer, it shows his picture. That way, no one can **compete** in the event **instead of** him!

[1] a **badge**

Reading Comprehension

A Circle the correct answer.

Detail **1.** Who ran in the Beijing torch relay?

   a. David   **b.** David's dad   **c.** a family friend

Inference **2.** In the first paragraph, which of these facts surprised David?

   a. The Beijing torch relay was the longest torch relay ever.
   b. The torches contain gas containers.
   c. Runners can keep their torches.

Vocabulary **3.** Which of these also uses a **rail** (line 13)?

   a. a ship   **b.** a train   **c.** a plane

Detail **4.** Which of these statements about Gabe Gardner is NOT true?

   a. He is an Olympic athlete.
   b. He had a badge with a computer chip.
   c. David asked him to come to a party.

B **Strategy: Identifying fact and opinion.** Which of these statements about the Olympics are facts (**F**) and which are opinions (**O**)?

   a. _____ David was very lucky.

   b. _____ The athletes have badges so only they can compete.

   c. _____ The Beijing Olympic torch is beautiful.

   d. _____ On TV, you can't see all the cameras at the Olympics.

   e. _____ David met Gabe Gardner in Beijing.

Language Practice

A Vocabulary: Completion. Complete the sentences using a word from the box.

> contains   record   compete   athletes   return   remove   instead of   official

1. At the Olympics, when you have a problem, you should ask a(n) _____ .

2. The _____ for the 100m men's running race is less than 10 seconds.

3. Soccer players have to _____ their watches[1] before a game.

4. Tennis players, swimmers, and runners are all _____ .

5. Many people watch sports _____ competing themselves.

6. An Olympic swimming pool[2] _____ about 2.5 million liters of water.

7. In a volleyball game, the two teams _____ to get 25 points.

8. After the Olympics, athletes _____ to their home countries.

[1] a **watch**

[2] a **swimming pool**

B Grammar: The prefix *re-*. Read these sentences; **b** is from the passage.

> **a.** But they can't **light** them **again**.   **b.** But they can't **relight** them.

Rewrite the sentences using a word with *re-*.

1. Do this again. _____

2. Write this again. _____

3. Read the passage again. _____

4. Tell the story again. _____

5. Start the computer again. _____

Usage

Record can have two meanings:
1. (n.) /ˈrekɔːd/ e.g. **a world** record, a record **player**
2. (v.) /rɪˈkɔːd/ e.g. record **a song**, record **some information**

chariot

spectators

horse

Olympia, Greece

▲ The first Olympic Games were in Olympia, Greece, in 776 B.C. At first, they lasted only one day. The chariot race was one of the most popular events.

Before You Read

A **Discussion.** Look at the picture and information above. How do you think the ancient Olympics were different than the modern ones? Talk with a partner.

B **Definitions.** Match the words with their meanings.

1. cheat **2.** crowd **3.** honest **4.** join **5.** promise **6.** quiet **7.** share **8.** voice

____ **a.** e.g. to look at another student's answers during a test

____ **b.** saying and doing only true things

____ **c.** to say you will do something

____ **d.** a big group of people

____ **e.** not noisy

____ **f.** to come or put together

____ **g.** to give part of something to someone

____ **h.** the sound we hear when someone talks

◄ Athletes running at the ancient Olympics. In this event, they wore heavy armor.

armor

runners

▼ Spectators watching wrestlers in the ancient Olympics. In most events, athletes competed without clothes.

wrestlers

spectators

Reading

Strategy: Skimming.
This passage is a story about the ancient Olympics. Who is the writer of the passage?

a. a spectator

b. an athlete

c. an official

Read the passage and check your answer.

LET THE GAMES BEGIN!

1   It was the first morning of the Olympic Games. We went to the stadium for the running races. Even though it was very early, **it** was already full of athletes. Some exercised, and some **stretched**. All of the athletes wanted to be ready for their games.

5   Other athletes were on the field. There were spectators all around them. As we **joined** the **crowd**, we heard trumpets[1] and the sounds of horses. The **voices** of the great crowds joined these sounds. I **shared** the excitement everyone felt.

As we watched, the athletes walked to the center of the field. The king wanted to know the athletes were good and **honest**. They **promised** not

10   to **cheat**. Then, one of the king's officials stood up. He asked the spectators, "Can anyone say anything bad about any of these athletes?"
It was very **quiet**. No one answered. After a minute, we heard, "Then let the games begin!"

[1] a **trumpet**

Reading Comprehension

A Circle the correct answer.

Inference **1.** In line 2, what does **it** refer to?

    a. the morning   **b.** the stadium   **c.** the race

Vocabulary **2.** What were the athletes **stretching** (line 3)?

    a. their horses   **b.** other athletes   **c.** their arms and legs

Inference **3.** Why did the official ask the spectators a question?

    a. The king didn't want athletes to cheat.
    b. He wanted spectators to enjoy themselves.
    c. He wanted to make the games more exciting.

Detail **4.** Which of these does the passage NOT talk about?

    a. what the athletes did before the games started
    b. who won the first race
    c. what the spectators saw and heard

B **Strategy: Sequencing.** Number the events in order from **1** to **6**.

    a. _____ The official asked the spectators a question.

    b. _____ The Olympic Games started.

    c. _____ The athletes promised to be honest.

    d. _____ Athletes competed in the running races.

    e. _____ The writer went to the stadium.

    f. _____ There was a noise of trumpets.

ancient Olympia ▶

Language Practice

A **Vocabulary: Words in context.** In each sentence, circle the best answer.

1. When you are (**honest** / **quiet**), you don't say untrue things.

2. It is hard not to touch people in a (**crowd** / **voice**).

3. During tests classrooms are usually (**honest** / **quiet**).

4. When you (**share** / **promise**) something, you say you will do it.

5. One way to become an athlete is to (**join** / **promise**) a soccer team.

6. Most lottery winners (**share** / **join**) the money they win with their family.

7. When one team in a game (**cheats** / **voices**), the other team isn't happy.

8. In a stadium full of spectators, you have to speak with a loud (**promise** / **voice**).

B **Grammar: *some, any, every, no*.** Read these sentences from the passage.

> **a.** He asked the spectators, "Can **anyone** say **anything** bad about **any** of these athletes?"
>
> **b.** **No one** answered.

Choose the best word to complete each question. Then ask and answer the questions with a partner.

1. Do you know (**everyone** / **anyone**) famous?

2. Do you think (**someone** / **everyone**) at the Olympics likes sports?

3. Are there any sports that (**everyone** / **everywhere**) in your family likes?

4. Did you ever put your keys[1] (**nowhere** / **somewhere**) and then forget where?

[1] a key

> ### Word Partners
> Use *promise* with:
> (n.) **break** a promise, **make** a promise, **keep** a promise
> (adj.) a **broken** promise, an **empty** promise, a **false** promise

The Olympics

A Preview. You will hear these words and phrases in the video.
Write the correct word below each picture.

> boxing   wrestling   weight   chariot

1. _____   2. _____   3. _____   4. _____

B After you watch. Which Olympics, ancient or modern, do these things match?
Write **a** to **h** in the correct place.

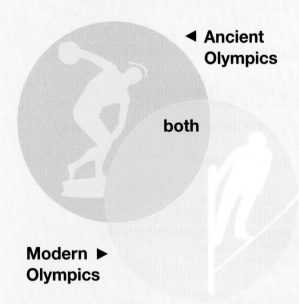

◀ **Ancient Olympics**

both

Modern ▶ Olympics

a. Athletes from all over the world come to compete.

b. The games are held every four years.

c. Men and women can compete in the games.

d. The winner gets an olive wreath.

e. Wrestling is an Olympic sport.

f. Boxers and wrestlers are divided into groups by weight.

g. Long jumpers hold weights in their hands to help them jump further.

h. The games are all held at Olympia.

C Think about it. How are the Olympics and the soccer World Cup similar and different?

Vocabulary Review

Crossword. Complete the crossword puzzle with words from Units 7 and 8.

Across

3. say you will do something
4. saying and doing only true things
6. give part of something to someone
7. to go in a sporting event
9. make something change
12. to take away, to take out
13. a big group of people or things

Down

1. came or was put together
2. people doing sports
3. good, +
5. almost the same
7. to make
8. to come back, take something back
10. to make something go in one way
11. the floor of a room, or the earth outside

World Heritage Notes

Notes Completion. Scan the information on pages 110 and 111 to complete the notes.

What: The Ruins of Ancient Olympia

Where: Olympia, _____

Data:

• Ancient Olympia has been a world heritage site since _____.

• People first lived in Olympia in the _____ century B.C.

• The city is famous for being the _____ of the Olympic Games.

• During the games, the Greek cities all stopped their _____ and made _____.

• Olympia is also famous as an important religious center.

• The ancient people built temples to the Greek god _____, and the goddess _____.

• The statue of Zeus was one of the seven _____ of the ancient world.

Olympia, Greece

Site: **The Ruins of Ancient Olympia**

Location: **Olympia, Greece**

Category: **Cultural**

Status: **World Heritage Site since 1989**

Olympia is an ancient city. People have lived there for thousands of years—since the 10th century B.C. As the birthplace of the Olympic Games, Olympia is famous for bringing people together to do amazing things. Every four years, the ancient Greeks stopped their wars and made peace for a short time, so their athletes could compete and focus on winning the games.

Today, the Olympics are no longer held in Olympia. The huge hippodrome created for the chariot and horse races is now gone. And instead of athletes, the stadium is often filled with crowds of tourists.

However, Olympia is not just famous for its games. In ancient times, it was also a very important religious center. The ancient Greeks built beautiful temples to their gods here—to Zeus, the king of the gods, and to the goddess Hera, his queen. Many people visited the area to bring gifts for the gods, and to ask them for good health, wealth, and happiness.

Today, the ruins of the stadium and temples remain to tell us the history of Olympia. The things scientists find here affect the way we understand the ancient Greeks.

The Lost Statue of Zeus

Around 432 B.C., a Greek artist named Pheidias made a statute of Zeus for the temple at Olympia. The statue was huge. At a record height of 12 meters, it was about seven times bigger than any other statue of Zeus at the time. The statue was made of bronze, gold, ivory, and various precious stones. It was so beautiful, people called it one of the seven wonders of the ancient world. People came from all over to see it. Sadly, in A.D. 393, it was removed from the temple and taken to Constantinople, and was later destroyed in the great fire of Lauseion, in A.D. 476.

A Greek Folktale

PERSEPHONE AND THE RETURN OF SPRING

1   Among the gods of ancient Greece, there was a beautiful goddess named Persephone. Persephone's father was Zeus, the king of the gods. Her mother was Demeter, the goddess of farms. The young goddess was lovely, like her mother. She smelled like roses. She loved to laugh and play.

5   One day, Persephone was playing with her friends in a field of flowers. Hades, the god of the Underworld, saw her and fell in love with her. He drove his chariot up through the ground and **grabbed** her. He took her to his kingdom below the Earth.

Demeter looked everywhere for her daughter, but could not find her. As she
cried, plants and trees around the world died. There was no food, and the
10 people became hungry. They cried to the gods, but no one could help. As
long as Demeter was sad, nothing would grow. Persephone was sad, too. The
Underworld was dark and cold, and she missed her mother. Finally, Zeus
made Hades let Persephone return to Earth. But first, Hades gave her four
pomegranate seeds to eat. Anyone who eats or drinks something from the
15 Underworld must live there forever. However, Persephone did not know the law,
and she ate the seeds.

So, for four months every year, Persephone returns to the Underworld. During
that time, Demeter is sad, so the ground is brown and nothing grows. Then, for
the next eight months, she lives on Earth. Then, everything grows again; the
20 fields are green and there's fruit in the trees.

Reading Comprehension

A **Reading Comprehension.** Circle the correct answer.

Detail **1.** Demeter is Persephone's _____.

        a. sister   **b.** mother   **c.** friend

Purpose **2.** Hades probably fell in love with Persephone because _____.

        a. she was playing in a field

        b. she liked the Underworld

        c. she was beautiful

Vocabulary **3.** In line 7, what does **grabbed** mean?

        a. touched   **b.** caught   **c.** lifted

Purpose **4.** Why does Persephone return to the Underworld every year?

        a. She wants to visit Hades.

        b. The ground on Earth is brown.

        c. She ate seeds in the Underworld.

B **Strategy: Sequencing.** Number the events in order from **1** to **5**.

    a. _____ Demeter could not find her daughter.

    b. _____ Persephone played with her friends.

    c. _____ Persephone returned to Earth for eight months.

    d. _____ Hades took Persephone to the Underworld.

    e. _____ Plants around the world died.

Vocabulary Extension

Vocabulary: Review. Circle the best word to complete each sentence.

1. (**Join** / **Share**) a sports team, practice hard, and one day maybe you can (**compete** / **examine**) in the Olympics.

2. (**Everyone** / **Anyone**) wants to (**save** / **contain**) money.

3. When you (**make** / **take**) a promise, you should (**keep** / **stay**) it.

4. It is a good idea to try to learn (**something** / **someone**) new (**any** / **every**) day.

5. Every day doctors save (**no one's** / **someone's**) (**life** / **lives**).

1 Volcanoes

Narrator: On Earth, there are about 1,500 active volcanoes. This means they still erupt.

About 90 percent of the volcanoes on Earth are near the Ring of Fire, around the Pacific Ocean.

The outside of the Earth is made from big pieces of rock, called plates. The plates move around a lot. When they move, rocks deep inside the Earth get hot. They become magma. When the magma comes out of a volcano, we call it lava.

In some volcanoes, the lava goes slowly down the side of the volcano. These volcanoes are safer to be near, and can be beautiful. Other times, a volcano's lava suddenly comes up from inside the Earth. The volcano erupts and rocks, ash, and lava go high into the air.

Kilauea, in Hawaii, is one of Earth's most active volcanoes. It has been erupting since 1983. People from all over the world go there to see it.

Kilauea's lava goes down the volcano and into the sea. Then it becomes new land.

But not all volcanoes are safe. In A.D. 79, Mount Vesuvius suddenly erupted near Pompeii in Italy. It was terrible. The ash went everywhere. The eruption of Mount Vesuvius killed 2,000 people.

Many volcanoes are not safe. But they can help us, too. Volcanoes made 80 percent of the land on Earth. They help plants to grow. They made a lot of the air, too.

Volcanoes help us understand the power deep inside the Earth.

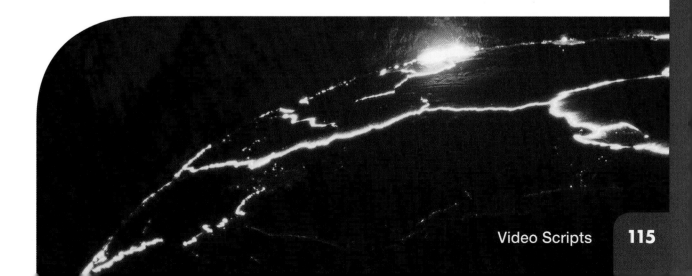

2 Cheetah vs. Gemsbok

Narrator: It's morning in the Kalahari Desert, in Africa.

A mother cheetah calls for her children. Where are they?

She can't find her cubs.

The two cheetah cubs are playing. They find a gemsbok in the grass.

It's alone, and hurt, and they are hungry.

The gemsbok is too big for them to kill. Even the mother cheetah cannot kill it.

The mother cheetah calls again, and the young cheetahs leave the gemsbok.

Cheetah mothers look after their cubs until they are more than a year old. Then the cubs will go away, and she will be alone again. When female cheetahs grow up, they usually live alone. But sometimes brothers like these stay together their whole lives.

The brothers run and play together, they also hunt together. Today, the brothers are hunting without their mother.

They find a lot of gemsbok.

The hunt begins.

The cubs catch a young gemsbok.

But the mother gemsbok sees that her child is in trouble.

And she is not happy. She doesn't want the cheetahs to kill her child.

She goes back to her child, and helps it.

The baby gemsbok is OK.

Now, the mother runs after the cheetahs. She wants them to go away.

The mother gemsbok can kill cheetahs, but today, she doesn't hurt them.

For now, the gemsbok can go home to their family, and the cheetah family is safe too.

It's the end of another day for the animals in the Kalahari.

3 An Amazing Trip

Narrator: Around the world, every child becomes an adult in a different way.

Yoro Sisse is a 16-year-old Fulani boy from Diafarabe, Mali. Every year, teams of young Fulani boys, like Yoro, make a long trip. They do this to find food for their cows.

During the dry season, the cows can stay near the Fulani's home. But in the wet season, there is too much rain for the cows to stay there. They take their cows into the Sahel, near the Sahara Desert. In the desert there aren't many trees or plants. It is very dry. The boys travel along the edge of the desert, moving from place to place.

The boys' trip can take almost eight months. There is little food for the boys near the desert. They do not carry a lot of food with them. They usually only drink milk.

Yoro: We have to keep moving to find more food for our cows. Our job is to bring back fat cows.

Narrator: This is something every Fulani boy has to do. It's a very important job. When Yoro goes home, everyone will look at his cows.

If the cows are all OK, the other Fulani people will know Yoro can take good care of his herd. Then, they will say he is not a boy, but a man.

This is Yoro's girlfriend, Aissa. She wants him to come back with good cows because she wants to marry him. In the Fulani tribe, mothers and fathers choose the person their children can marry. If Yoro doesn't come back with good cows, Aissa's parents won't let her marry him.

During the trip, Yoro thinks about many things. He worries about finding food for his cows. He also worries about other people who want to take the cows.

Yoro starts his journey in Diafarabe, Mali. He takes his cows through Mauritania, to the Sahel. The Fulani people have walked this way for thousands of years. Yoro has walked for three months. Now he is going back to his home—and his family, and his girlfriend.

Yoro: We walk all day without stopping. Sometimes we get very thirsty, and the cows get tired. Often, we don't sleep at night.

Narrator: The young cows in Yoro's herd look good. Everyone can see Yoro's hard work. He marks them so everyone knows they are his.

The trip is almost over, and Yoro is excited to see his girlfriend.

But, now they still have to cross the river. Yoro swims with his cows. He wants to make sure they are OK.

Across the river, his family and friends wait for the boys. After a long and difficult trip, Yoro's cows are all OK. It's time to celebrate and have fun.

4 Solar Cooking

Narrator: It's a cool day in Borrego Springs, California, but Eleanor Shimeall is cooking outside. She doesn't need electricity, wood, or gas. She's cooking with the energy of the sun.

Eleanor: I'm gonna check on this chicken and rice and see how it's . . . whether it's cooking. Ah, it's doing a good job.

Narrator: Eleanor started cooking with the sun almost 30 years ago. Using a machine called a solar cooker, she can cook meat, fish, and bread.

It is a slow way of cooking, but is both cheap and healthy. It's also good for the Earth.

In places where cooking with electricity is impossible, solar cookers can save lives. Eleanor is part of Solar Cookers International (SCI), a group showing people how to use the sun's energy in their daily lives.

In some places, women have to walk up to five kilometers every day to get wood. It's hard work. Then they make a fire. The smoke makes the air dirty. This dirty air is bad for the Earth and for humans.

SCI, and other groups want to help. So, they teach these families to use the sun to cook. Now, more than 30,000 families are cooking with the sun.

Wendy, Solar Cook: Oh, this is good. It's very good. The consistency is good, the texture is fine—no problem.

African villager: We're all amazed that a cardboard box can cook.

Narrator: SCI's solar cooker is easy to use. And it's very cheap. It's only $5. And, it lasts for two years. When people use the solar cooker, the dark pot and the plastic bags keep in the sun's energy.

The energy from the sun makes the dark pot hot so it can cook the food.
Solar energy can also clean water. Many people don't have safe drinking water. Dirty water can make people sick. Scientists say dirty water kills about 6,000 people every day.

But with solar energy, people don't need big machines to make clean water. They can just use a little solar cooker. This is a WAPI. It shows people when the water is hot enough. That way, the people know the water is clean, and safe to drink.

Solar power is becoming very useful and popular in many places. And SCI is working to get more people all over the world to use this cheap and clean energy.

African villager: OK, solar cooker!

5 Treasure Under My Home

Narrator: Egypt is famous for its treasures from the past. In Egypt, selling artifacts is illegal, but some people still do it. In some villages in Egypt, people's houses are right on top of tombs. It's easy for these people to find treasure. Dr. Fredrik Hiebert is an expert on Egyptian artifacts.

He says that some sellers of artifacts aren't thinking about what the artifacts can tell us about Egypt's amazing history. Lisa Ling is a famous reporter. Lisa wants to find out about the people selling these artifacts. She found out about a man selling artifacts illegally. She is going to meet this man.

Lisa: We're gonna be using this camera, and I don't really know what's going to happen from here on out, so as soon as he calls, we're going to go meet him on the street somewhere.

Narrator: Finally, Lisa goes to meet the man. She must meet him secretly, and she cannot show his face.

Lisa: Wow. So is that it? That's the tunnel?

Man: Yes.

Narrator: The man shows Lisa an old tunnel. It used to go to a tomb but now the artifacts are all gone.

Lisa: So it's really deep, huh?

Man: Yeah, it's too deep.

Lisa: Have you ever gone down there?

Man: Yeah, I've gone before.

Lisa: What this man is saying is that the poor people who live up here in upper Egypt, they really don't know so much about history and when they find something they see they can make money off it, so they sell it for food, is that right?

Man: Yeah.

Narrator: The man usually hides these items, but today, he shows them to Lisa. He says they are real artifacts. They are very old and very special. He says these were found under somebody's house.

Lisa: So do you sell these things?

Man: Yeah.

Lisa: How much do you think you could sell this for?

Man: Ten thousand dollars.

Lisa: So we're being told that all this stuff together is worth about 30 thousand U.S. dollars. It's incredible that this has survived thousands of years if this is in fact real. This is amazing. I've really never seen anything like these before.

Narrator: Egyptian smugglers can sell these items because people around the world want them. After they leave the country, it is very hard to get them back. But the police are trying to stop them. They are also trying to teach people not to sell their country's artifacts.

Dr. Hiebert says things are getting better. More people in Egypt are learning about their history. When these people find out more about their history, they want to keep these items safe, not sell them to smugglers. The smugglers are hard to catch, but the police and experts want to stop them and protect Egypt's wonderful artifacts, and its rich history.

6 Plants

Narrator: Across the world, plants and animals need each other to live. Plants grow almost everywhere on the planet. In the center of the desert, in the Arctic. And even in the ocean. Scientists today know over 250,000 kinds of plants, and they think there are many more plants that we don't know anything about.

Green plants are important for all living things because plants make their own food. The food that plants make becomes food for us all. Green plants take carbon dioxide, water, and sunlight, and use these to make food.

Then some animals, like these ants, eat the plants. And then meat-eating animals eat those animals. So, in the end, plants feed everyone. We also need plants because when plants make food, they make new oxygen.

This oxygen helps make the air we breathe. But plants need animals, too. Flowers aren't just beautiful to look at. They have different colors because small animals, like insects, like the colors and sweet smells. They go to the flowers to get food.

That's good for the animals, but it also helps the plants. Plants need birds and insects to help carry their pollen to several other plants. This helps the flowers to make new flowers. Other animals like birds and bats often help the flowers, too.

Sometimes, animals and insects are useful to plants as food. This pitcher plant is slippery inside. Small insects land inside it and cannot get out. Then, they die and the plant eats them.

Another plant that eats insects is the sundew. Insects come to the sundew because it looks nice. When the insect touches the sundew, it sticks to the plant, and can't escape.

Plants use animals to move their seeds too. Animals come to eat the plant's fruit. Then they carry the plant's seeds to other places where the plant can grow.

Sometimes when an animal eats the fruit, the seeds fall on the ground. And small animals pick up the seeds—and cover them with dirt. Some of these seeds then grow into little plants. Later, the baby plant will become a big tree, starting the cycle again.

7 The Solar System

Narrator: Our Solar System is in the Milky Way Galaxy. Scientists say that it was created four and a half billion years ago. A big cloud of dust and gases slowly flattened and became hot. This finally made a new star, our sun. There are eight main planets going around our sun. These planets and the sun together are called our Solar System. The sun is in the center. It's so big it's 100 times heavier than all the planets together.

The closest planet to the sun is Mercury. In the day, it's very hot—about 400 degrees Celsius. At night, it's very cold—about minus 180 degrees Celsius.

Next is Venus. Venus is about the same size as Earth. But its air is mostly made of carbon dioxide, a gas that keeps heat in. So Venus is always very hot. The temperature on Venus is nearly 500 degrees Celsius, so people cannot go there.

The third planet from the sun is Earth. More than 70% of the Earth is covered with water. A lot of scientists think Earth is the only planet with life on it. Some are still looking for life on other planets.

After Earth, there is Mars. It's called the red planet because the ground is covered with red dirt. Mars has the deepest canyon and the tallest mountain in the whole Solar System.

Then there are a lot of asteroids. Most of them are less than two kilometers wide.

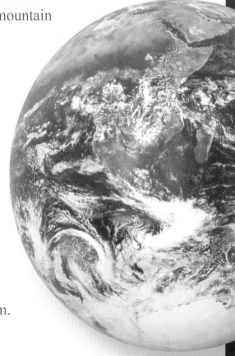

Jupiter is the largest planet in the Solar System, more than 1,300 times bigger than Earth. It has a stormy, red spot. This stormy area is twice as wide as Earth.

Saturn is next. It's the second largest planet. Its famous rings are made of ice. Similar to Jupiter, Saturn is made mostly of gas.

The seventh planet from the sun is Uranus. It has rings, too, and at least 27 moons!

Neptune, the eighth planet, is the windiest place in the Solar System. It's the last planet, but it's not the end of the Solar System.

After Neptune, there's Pluto. Scientists think Pluto is too small to be called a planet. Today, we call Pluto a dwarf planet.

Our Solar System is amazing, but there are many other suns and planets in our galaxy for scientists to focus on and study. And there are billions of galaxies out there!

8 The Olympics

Narrator: Every four years, athletes from all over the world compete in the Olympic games.

The first Olympic games were held more than two thousand seven hundred years ago. Like today, the games then were held every four years. In those days, only men could compete in the games.

They came from all over Greece, to the city of Olympia, to see who was the best.

Instead of having many types of sports, when the games began, there was just one competition—the footrace.

According to legend, the first Olympic champion was a cook named Coreobus. He ran in a 192 meter race, surrounded by huge crowds of people.

During the games, all athletes and officials made a promise to be fair, and honest. If any athlete cheated, he was removed from the competition, and had to pay the officials money.

Soon, there were more events. We can still see some of these sports in the Olympics today.

The discus throw then was similar to today's sport. But the ancient Greeks threw a large flat rock, while today's discuses are usually metal.

Ancient long jumpers held weights in their hands to help them jump further.

The javelin was a long wooden pole thrown across a stadium. These ancient javelins were mostly identical to the ones used today, except for a leather finger hold which helped the ancients throw further.

The ancient Greeks also held horse-riding and chariot-racing competitions. These races were dangerous, but the crowd loved them.

Another sport was wrestling. To win a wrestling match, one athlete had to throw the other down three times.

In boxing, matches then didn't stop until one athlete gave up, or couldn't get up again. Today, boxers and wrestlers are divided into different groups based on weight. But in ancient Greece, amazingly, for boxing and wrestling, there were just two groups. One for men, and the other, for boys.

For each sport, there was only one winner.

That person got an olive wreath to show that they won. When they returned home, everyone loved them. They were famous, and shared their fame with their hometowns.

Then, in A.D. 393—after almost twelve centuries—the Roman emperor Theodosius the First put an end to the Olympics.

But, of course, that wasn't really the end. In 1894, officials from 10 different countries met to organize the first modern Olympics. Two years later, in 1896, the Olympics began again.

And since then, the Olympic games have become more popular than ever.

Indexes

Target Vocabulary Index

Reading Strategy Index

Grammar Index

Photo Credits

1 Carsten Peter/NGIC, **3** Frans Lanting/NGIC, **4** (t to b) Kent Fredriksson/Zenfolio, Jim Richardson/NGIC, Mark Foley/AP Photo, Mark Moffett/Minden Pictures/NGIC, **5** (t to b) Richard Nowitz/NGIC, Lorina Barbalas, (l) Michael Nichols/NGIC, (c) Michael S. Yamashita/NGIC, (r) Joel Sartore/NGIC, **6, 7** (t, l to r) Jim Richardson/NGIC, Richard Nowitz/NGIC, Scala/Art Resource, Helene Schmitz/NGIC, Tim Laman/NGIC, Martin Kraft/Shutterstock, Robert Clark/NGIC, David Fisher/NGIC, Martin Gray/NGIC, Michael Nichols/NGIC, Carsten Peter/NGIC, Joel Sartore/NGIC, J. Bell (Cornell U.) and M. Wolff (SSI)/NASA, Renee Comet/NGIC, **11** Carsten Peter/NGIC, **12** John Stanmeyer LLC/NGIC, **13** (t to b) John Stanmeyer LLC/NGIC, Carsten Peter/NGIC, John Stanmeyer LLC/NGIC, **14** John Stanmeyer LLC/NGIC, **15** N Mrtgh/Shutterstock, **16** Grafissimo/iStockphoto, pictore/iStockphoto, **19** (t) Alexxl/Shutterstock, (b) Viktor Gmyria/Shutterstock, **21** Tim Laman/NGIC, **22–24** (all photos) Michael Nichols/NGIC, **26** (t) Joel Sartore/NGIC, (b) Yva Momatiuk & John Eastcott/Minden Pictures/NGIC, **27** (t) AlaskaStock, (b) Kent Fredriksson/Zenfolio, **28** Joel Sartore/NGIC, **29** irin-k/Shutterstock, **30** (l) EcoPrint/Shutterstock, (r) Magnus Haese/Shutterstock, **31** (t) Mark C. Ross/NGIC, (b) Greg801/iStockphoto, **31–32** (spread) Kevin Smith/NGIC, **33** (t, b) Jim Williams, NASA GSFC Scientific Visualization Studio, and the Landsat 7 Science Team, **37** Robert Madden/NGIC, **38** (t to b) Michael S. Yamashita/NGIC, Martin Kraft/Shutterstock, Jon Helgason/iStockphoto, AnatolyM/Shutterstock, **39** (t) Michael S. Yamashita/NGIC, (b) E.H. Wilson/NGIC **41** Michael S. Yamashita/NGIC, **42** Richard Nowitz/NGIC, **43** (t to b) Kenneth Garrett/NGIC, Martin Gray/NGIC, **45** (t to b) tatniz/Shutterstock, Alexandr Makarov/Shutterstock, **46** National Geographic, **47** Tim Laman/NGIC, **48** David Fisher/NGIC, **49** (t) Smar Jodha/NGIC, (b) Lev Kropotov/Shutterstock, **52** (clockwise from tl to br) Mark Thiessen/NGIC, Mark Thiessen/NGIC, Rebecca Hale/NGIC, Jan Danel/Shutterstock, **53** (t to b) Renee Comet/NGIC, Alison Kuhlmann, **56** (1) Rebecca Hale/NGIC, (2) Stacy Gold/NGIC, (3) Shawn Hempel/Shutterstock, (4) Jodi Cobb/NGIC, **57** (t) James L. Stanfield/NGIC, (b) Greg801/iStockphoto, **58–59** James L. Stanfield/NGIC, **63** Bill Curtsinger/NGIC, **64** Steve McCurry/Magnum/NGIC, **65** (tl to b) Charles O'Rear/NGIC, Mark Foley/AP Photo, Claudia Veja/Shutterstock, **67** koya979/Shutterstock, **68** Jonathan Blair/NGIC, **69** (t) Jeffrey Dunn/WBGH, (all bl to r) Brendan Hunter/iStockphoto, **72** (l to r) Kenneth Garrett/NGIC, Victor R. Boswell, Jr./NGIC, **73** Helene Schmitz/NGIC, **74** (tr) Helene Schmitz/NGIC, **75** (t to b) Helene Schmitz/NGIC, Joel Sartore/NGIC, Helene Schmitz/NGIC, (bl to r) Ryby/Shutterstock, Bogdan Ionescu/Shutterstock, **76** (l to r) Helene Schmitz/NGIC, Joel Sartore/NGIC, Helene Schmitz/NGIC, **77** (t to b) Tatuasha/Shutterstock, Photos.com/GettyImages, **78** (l to r) Joel Sartore/NGIC, Robert Clark/NGIC, **79** Greg801/iStockphoto, **80** (br) Cisca Castelijns/Foto Natura/Minden Pictures/NGIC, **81** (t to b) Photostudio 7/Shutterstock, Kurhan/Shutterstock, Yuri Arcurs/Shutterstock, **82** (t to b) (1) Roy Toft/NGIC, (2) Heidi & Hans-Jurgen Koch/Minden Pictures/NGIC, (b, l to r) National Geographic, Cathy Keifer/Shutterstock, National Geographic, National Geographic, **83** (t to b) Frans Lanting/NGIC, Nigel Hicks/NGIC, Frans Lanting/NGIC, Greg801/iStockphoto, **84–85** (main) Frans Lanting/NGIC, **84** (b) Nigel Hicks/NGIC, **85** (t to b) Joel Sartore/NGIC, Frans Lanting/NGIC, Mark Moffett/Minden Pictures/NGIC, **89** Jim Richardson/NGIC, **90** Jim Richardson/NGIC, **91** (t and b) Jim Richardson/NGIC, **92** Jim Richardson/NGIC, **94** (r) NASA Jet Propulsion Laboratory, **95** (b) NASA/NGIC, **96** (l) NASA, J. Bell (Cornell U.) and M. Wolff (SSI)/NGIC, (r) NASA/NGIC, **97** Sascha Burkard/Shutterstock,

99 Cameron Lawson/NGIC, **100** Amy Sancetta/AP Photo, **101** (all) Lorina Barbalas, **102** Aija Lehtonen/Shutterstock, **103** (t) Photos.com/Getty Images, (b) Maryunin Yury Vasilevich/Shutterstock, **105** (b) Photos.com/Getty Images, **107** Photos.com/Getty Images, **108** (l to r) Stockbyte/Thinkstock, Janie Airey/Thinkstock, iStockphoto/Thinkstock, Thomas Northcut/Thinkstock, **109** (t) Netfalls/Shutterstock, (b) Greg801/iStockphoto, **110–111** Netfalls/Shutterstock, **115** Carsten Peter/NGIC, **117** National Geographic, **119** Rebecca Hale/NGIC, **121** Victor R. Boswell, Jr./NGIC, **122** NASA, J. Bell (Cornell U.) and M. Wolff (SSI)/NGIC, **123** NASA/NGIC, **125** (t) Aija Lehtonen/Shutterstock, (b) Stockbyte/Thinkstock

Illustration Credits

12 (t, r), **15** (t), **17, 20** (all), **22, 26, 30, 32, 42, 46, 72, 84, 104** (b), **110**, National Geographic Maps, **5** Tom Lovell/NGIC, **7** EugenP/Shutterstock, **12** (l) EugenP/Shutterstock, (r) Page2 LLC, **16** (b), **17–18** Eric Foenander, **23** (lr) Page2 LLC, **27** Page2 LLC, **34–35** Eric Foenander, **38** National Geographic Maps, **42** (t) AnatolyM/Shutterstock, (b) sellingpix/Shutterstock, **43** (t) Payne, C.F./NGIC, **50** Hiram Henriquez/NGIC, **52** Redmirage/Shutterstock, **58** National Geographic Maps, **60–61** Eric Foenander, **66** zentilia/Shutterstock, **70** (bl) Page2 LLC, **74** (tl) Jenny Wang/NGIC, **79** (tr) Jenny Wang/NGIC, (bl) Page2 LLC, **80** (tr) Jenny Wang/NGIC, **84** (c) National Geographic Maps, **86–87** Eric Foenander, **94–95** (t) NGIC, **94** (cl) Leremy/Shutterstock, (b) Sellingpix/Shutterstock (r) Kounadeas Ioannhs/Shutterstock, **98** NASA/JPL/Caltech, **100** National Geographic Maps, **104** (t) H.M. Herget/NGIC, **105** (tl and tr) Tom Lovell/NGIC, **106** Pierers Universal-Lexikon, **108** (b) Page2 LLC, **111** Duncan Walker/iStockphoto, **112–113** Eric Foenander

Text Credits

13 Adapted from "The Gods Must Be Restless: Living in the Shadow of Indonesia's Volcanoes," by Andrew Marshal: NGM, January 2008, **17** Adapted from "Journey to the Center of the Earth," by Jules Verne (1864), **23** Adapted from "Life with Father," by Ian Nichols: NGM, August 2004, **27** Adapted from "Animal Love: Do Animal Siblings Care About Each Other?" by Aline Alexander Newman: NGK, February 2008, **35** Adapted from "The Hare and the Water," retold by Gary Porter, http://www.peacecorps.gov/wws/educators/enrichment/africa/lessons/ESlang02/Eslang02sup02.pdf, **39** Adapted from "China's Tea Horse Road," by Mark Jenkins: NGM, May 2010, **43** Adapted from "The Pyramid Builders," by Virginia Morell: NGM, November 2001, **49** Adapted from "Dubai's Rotating Skyscraper," by Winona Dimeo-Ediger: NGM, February 2009, **53** Adapted from "Big Ideas, Little Packages," by Margaret G. Zackowitz: NGM, November 2010, **61** Traditional tale, **69** Adapted from "You Could Already Be a Millionaire!" by Kristen Baird Rattini: NGK, March 2005, **75** Adapted from "Fatal Attraction: Carnivorous Plants," by Carl Zimmer: NGM, March 2010, **79** Adapted from "Insectivorous Plants," by Charles Darwin (1875), **87** Adapted with permission from "Earth Care: World Folktales to Talk About," by Margaret Read MacDonald, © 1999, August House Publishers, Inc., **91** Adapted from "Our Vanishing Night: Light Pollution," by Verlyn Klinkenborg: NGM, November 2008, **101** Adapted from "You Are Here: Beijing," National Geographic Kids Website, http://kidsblogs.nationalgeographic.com/you-are-here/beijing/, **105** Adapted from "Festivals, Games, and Amusements: Ancient and Modern," by Horace Smith and Samuel Woodworth (1832), **112–113** Traditional tale

National Geographic Image Collection = NGIC
National Geographic Kids Magazine = NGK
National Geographic Magazine = NGM